ONLINE MEETINGS THAT MATTER

Online Meetings that Matter
A guide for managers of remote teams

ISBN 978-0-9572802-4-3 (Print edition)

British Library Cataloguing-in-Publication data

A catalogue record for this book is available from the British Library

The purpose of this book is to provide the reader with general information about the subject matter presented. This book is for inspiration purposes only. This book is not intended, nor should the user consider it, to be legal advice for a specific situation.

The author, company, and publisher make no representations or warranties with respect to the accuracy, fitness, completeness, or applicability of the contents of this book. The author, company, and publisher shall in no event be held liable for any loss or other damages, including but not limited to special, incidental, consequential, or other damages. Please consider carefully any advice the authors give before applying it in your workplace.

If you would like to tweet or share online any of the illustrations, feel free to visit www.onlinemeetingsthatmatter.com

Cover design: Manuel Barrio

Design: Simon Hartshorne

Illustrations: Pilar Orti

ONLINE MEETINGS THAT MATTER

A GUIDE FOR MANAGERS OF REMOTE TEAMS

Pilar Orti

Contents

Preface

Communicating with team members through technology is no longer the domain of employees working in global teams in multinationals. As people choose to work from home (or as companies decide that their employees should work from home) or from locations that don't involve a commute, we are spending less and less time in the same physical space as our team members. Gathering talent from across the country or the world is possible, even for those businesses with limited budgets.

As we get used to interacting with our colleagues through technology, it is only natural that we should have more conversations online, and begin to hold meetings in the online space. In one way, online meetings are no different to 'in the flesh' meetings – those we are used to holding in the office with our colocated colleagues, and which have gained a bad reputation in the workplace. But in another way, online meetings are events of a different kind.

A STEP IN THE RIGHT DIRECTION

I hadn't realised the importance of online meetings in creating a more flexible work set-up until I talked to my friend, Sue. Sue is in charge of operations and facilities at a traditional organisation that recently moved into a new building. Given that they needed to move to new premises, they had to change how they were working as an organisation. The new building was designed as an activity-based workplace, giving people the option to work from wherever in the building suited their task or activity best: quiet areas for high-focus tasks, collaborative areas for interactive tasks, and so on. In addition, the company started to enable people to work from home.

When I mentioned to Sue that I was writing a book about online meetings, she said: "We most definitely need that! The other day I was talking to one of our directors, whose biggest worry was that if people started to work from home, they could never find the time to meet as a team."

By moving team meetings online, we can get rid of many concerns and objections to 'going remote', such as 'We'll never be able to arrange a meeting.' This concern, together with loss of team spirit, makes many managers and business leaders nervous about freeing people up to work from wherever they work best.[1] It's a concern which can be easily addressed.

THEY ARE THE SAME, BUT DIFFERENT

While online meetings can work, it is hard to pretend that attending them is the same as meeting with people in a room. Even when we are on video and can see all of our team members, we interact in two dimensions, not three.[2] Our world suddenly becomes flat. We see our colleagues in front of us on a flat screen, sitting symmetrically next to each other in little boxes. Our necks become stiff, as there is no need to move our heads from side-to-side to look at the different people around us. We become talking heads rather than people.

Some ways in which we build rapport with each other, such as sharing a quick glance, are lost. Sometimes they are replaced by typing in the chat box, or commenting on what someone is saying by making some larger-than-life gesture. And if we are unlucky, one of us will have a bad internet connection that creates unnatural gaps in our conversation.

Yes, online meetings take some getting used to, but their essence is no different to that of those we hold when we are in the same space.

We meet to:

- **discuss** our work
- **share** information
- **support** one another
- **challenge** one another
- generate **ideas**
- **troubleshoot**
- speed up a **decision**-making process
- **review** our progress
- **learn.**

---

1 Let's face it, not being able to see people working hard at their computer is also a concern for some managers, but addressing this is beyond the scope of this book.

2 Although watch out: virtual reality is coming soon to a workplace near you!

On top of all that, in the online world meetings take on another, important function: **socialising**.

SOCIAL ANIMALS

In the colocated workplace (that is, where we share the same location), socialising takes place spontaneously in corridors, during coffee breaks, at lunchtime, when you walk past someone's desk on the way to the toilet, or outside on the way home from the office. This means that when we take time out from our day-to-day tasks to attend a meeting, we want to get down to business straightaway.

In the online world, although there are ways of nurturing these social interactions, meetings can be key to increasing connection and decreasing isolation, especially when team members are working from home. In virtual teams where employees are located in different company offices, it is easy for people to feel less connected to their virtual colleagues than to those they see in the office every day.

Even though meetings often have a terrible reputation in the workplace, this is why they are worth transferring to the online space – as long as we run them mindfully, with a purpose in mind, and periodically review the value they bring to our team.

There is also a highly practical aspect to getting used to meeting online: we become comfortable using technology and having conversations with others in this way. We might take this for granted when everything is going well in our team, when we are completely in sync with each other and when no external forces disrupt our work. But when things go wrong, there are signs of miscommunication or we fall behind with our work, it is valuable to know that we can easily hop on a video call to:

- Talk to each other
- Make sure we aren't misinterpreting those messages posted in the middle of the night
- Make sure that miscommunication around tasks doesn't result in breakdown of relationships.

Nowadays, it isn't uncommon for the first interview with a new candidate, potential client or current customer to take place over video. What better way to be always prepared for high-stakes meetings than to be at ease with talking online with your team members?

MOVING ON

Of course, many global corporations have been running virtual meetings since the 1990s. These meetings mostly took the form of audio conferences, and many still do. The transition within those companies to video has been slow, and frequently included the use of high-end technology such as Cisco Telepresence or other screens to give a feeling of being surrounded by others, instead of the more affordable and accessible combination of headset–webcam, and free or low-cost meeting platforms, that small businesses and start-ups have embraced.

The arguments for meeting in-person – such as the fact that body language is important[3] in communication, or that it's easier to create a healthy meeting rhythm if we see each other – does not always hold when we consider that some of our non-verbal communication comes from tone of voice, and that video can help us pick up a great deal of visual information.

Even though I was tempted to focus the book on video meetings and address audio meetings only in a dedicated chapter, the above facts (together with feedback from readers) pushed me to cover both audio-only and video calls. Personal preferences and poor access to stable technology also mean that the audio-only experience still has a place in a book talking about team online meetings.

Having said that, I still believe that as an increasing number of organisations talk about having a 'mobile workforce', and as more

---

3   Mehrabian statistics about how we communicate are often misquoted, putting non-verbal communication way above verbal communication in all situations. Mehrabian's research showed that we absorb information through these channels: words 7%, tone of voice 38% and body language 55%. However, these statistics come from situations when the receiver feels that there is some inconsistency in the message communicated. Businessballs (2019) 'Mehrabian's communication theory: Verbal, non-verbal, body language'. Available at: www.businessballs.com/communication-skills/mehrabians-communication-theory-verbal-non-verbal-body-language/. (For a rant on this, check out Virtual Not Distant (2016) 'Myths that get in the way of embracing virtual teamwork', podcast, 8 March. Available at: www.virtualnotdistant.com/podcasts/myths.)

telecommunication companies make widely available fibre broadband a priority, video meetings will become more common. The main barrier to great video meetings is not a 'bad hair day', or people wanting to hide that they are carrying out email correspondence as you talk; it's an unstable internet connection – a hurdle we might overcome soon.

DON'T OVERDO IT

While I have written this book to encourage you to have regular meetings with your remote team, I am not suggesting that online meetings take up all of your time. One advantage of working remotely is that we can design our schedule to work without interruptions for decent chunks of time. Meetings shouldn't impede this: they should support all our other collaboration efforts.

While people have not been running online meetings for as long as colocated ones, they already have a bad name. For a start, they are called 'teleconferences' or 'something-conference', which makes them sound too formal and impersonal. Conferences tend to involve events where the flow of communication is one-to-many. It's time we stopped calling our team meetings 'teleconferences' or 'video conferences', when all we are doing is having a conversation.

Online meetings also have a bad name, because tech-enabled meetings were around for decades when the technology wasn't that great. If you experienced teleconferences in the late 1990s, you will visualise people gathered around a spider phone, talking to others who sound far away, rather than picturing people in different locations chatting to one another with a wireless headset, or even from their mobile phone, as they catch up with each other in a 21st-century manner.

Finally, meetings have a bad reputation because people are forced (or feel forced) to attend them. And when we feel like people would rather be somewhere else, those of us running the meetings feel responsible for entertaining everyone present. We begin to worry more about whether people are engaged in the meeting, rather than whether we are achieving what we set out to do.[4]

---

4   Interestingly, sometimes the fear of no one turning up to a meeting can be greater than fearing that people will be disengaged during it – this prevents managers from making them optional. In *Why Work Sucks*, the authors have 13 principles by which a 'Results Only

WHO THIS BOOK IS FOR

This book is for you if you are the manager or leader of a non-colocated team, where working schedules overlap for several hours, ideally by no less than four.[5] By 'non-colocated', I mean teams whose members rarely gather together in the office: virtual teams, remote teams, flexible set-ups (including working from home), distributed teams or dispersed workers.

Purists might say that there is a distinction between all those terms: I think they have gradually become interchangeable, and soon they will become dispensable. We'll only speak of 'teams'.

You might be making the transition to flexible working or 'agile working', and finding that your usual meeting schedule and formats are no longer possible, because you cannot gather everyone together in the same room.

You might be worried also about people's work becoming misaligned, losing team spirit, and people feeling disconnected from the work, the organisation and from one another – so you've moved some of your team meetings online.

You might be a new manager, getting ready for your first online team meeting; you might be an aspiring manager, discovering what your job might entail. Or maybe you are a team member who understands the potential of online meetings, and wants to make sure your team makes the most out of them.

You might even be a meeting facilitator or a coach, looking for ways to help teams and managers take ownership of their online meetings.

And if you are someone who organises meetings for online communities, you will find aspects of this book relevant too.

Finally, this book is for you if your team both *needs* and *wants* to gather together online. Some teams are happy to communicate on a one-to-one basis or through text, but if you think gathering together online as a team

---

Work Environment' should abide. When they tried to implement these in the company Best Buy, they found that the principle generating most resistance from management was 'Every meeting is optional'. Cali Ressler and Jody Thompson (2011) *Why Work Sucks and How to Fix It: The Results-Only Revolution*, Portfolio, p. 89.

5   In their book, *From Chaos to Successful Distributed Agile Teams*, the authors recommend an overlap of four hours to make sure that team members do not end up staying up too late in the day, or getting up too early, to make a meeting. Johanna Rothman and Mark Kilby (2019) *From Chaos to Successful Distributed Agile Teams: Collaborate to Deliver*, Practical Ink.

will help you to advance the work and create collaborative relationships, I invite you to continue reading.

THAT PERFECT MEETING

Guess what? We're all different, and so a perfect meeting will look and feel different to different people.

Some of you will leave a meeting satisfied when you have put together an action plan or resolved a miscommunication. Some will enjoy those meetings where you can reconnect with team members through sharing your latest blunder, and laughing about it together. My aim is that throughout this book you will identify those practices that help you make meetings both a useful component of your ongoing team communication, and a productive component of your overall communication ecosystem.

To help with this, I have included 'Inspiration' examples, where I describe practices in distributed organisations. When reading these, always ask yourself:

- What would need to change for this to work in my team?
- Why specifically do I think this might never work for us?

"BUT SOME OF THIS IS APPLICABLE TO REAL LIFE…"

As you read through this book, you might say to yourself: "But this is applicable not only to online meetings, it's relevant to those in 'real life." Well, online meetings *are* real life. I could even describe meeting over video to be meeting 'in-person', because we are virtually there: present.

I have gathered stories and practices about meetings from a range of different companies, and drawn advice from a wide range of books, not all focusing on the online space. In addition, I have shared some of my own experiences as virtual team member, manager of a distributed team, and team coach and trainer. Putting this book together has helped me dissect my own practice and reconsider some advice I have been giving up until now. Writing this book has been quite a challenge, as I have always resisted giving people tips and advice: I much prefer to ask teams and individuals questions that will help them come up with answers they can explore in their own context.

We can transfer much of what we have learned about great colocated meetings to the online space, but we need to unpack what works and implement it deliberately. If not, we can miss out on some practices that do transfer online, and end up with online meetings that don't seem to go anywhere.

When we meet online we are still meeting people, but we need to behave in slightly different ways – and it takes time to get used to that. Some of you, my dear readers, will love it. You'll love:

- Not having to include 'buffer time' to get to and from a meeting
- Knowing that you will be on time, because you don't have to travel across town
- Hearing the birds singing in somebody else's garden
- Seeing your colleagues in the middle of a lonely day from the comfort of your own home

Conversely, some of you will never warm to online meetings. You will crave to get away from the screen; you will long for the days when you met in-person around a table. And there is a group of you who don't like meetings, period: neither online nor off. If either of these apply to you, I hope that at least this book will help you to discover a few things to make your experience just that bit more comfortable.

Throughout this book I will talk about 'going to' your online meetings. Even though you might not be leaving your physical location to meet up, you will need to travel through cyberspace. Plus you will need to shift your mindset from working on your own to being with others; and if you are hopping from one meeting to the other, you will move from working with one set of people to working with another. Saying that you are 'going to a meeting' might help with that mindset shift.

ARE YOU READY?

Running meetings that matter requires understanding not only how to work with the technology involved, but also knowing how meetings fit into your wider team practice, as well as how they affect the relationships in your team.

Part 1: Your Ecosystem looks at the processes to include in your team communication ecosystem, and how they can work alongside your meetings.

Part 2: Relationships focuses on running meetings to strengthen relationships in your team. (This section also advocates for a non-hierarchical approach and reminds us that as people, we have all sorts of different needs.)

Part 3: The Meeting concentrates on the more practical aspects of planning and running the meeting.

At the end of Parts 2 and 3 you will find chapters covering specific meeting formats, including one on hybrid meetings for those teams which are located together in the office, but have some remote colleagues.

Part 4: The Kit is dedicated to the set-up and technology needed to run your meetings, as well as how to navigate broadband problems and choose an appropriate meeting platform.

To help you reflect on how the content of the book can be used in your team, each chapter ends with some questions under the heading 'Make your meetings matter'.

I THOUGHT I WAS READY, BUT...

Writing *Online Meetings that Matter* has been an interesting experience. I meet regularly with people over video, and meeting others online is part of my everyday life. When I work with managers and teams still unfamiliar with the online space, I realise that sometimes I forget what it was like to sit in front of a camera and feel exposed, uncomfortable or unnatural.

In writing this book, I have had to dissect many of the behaviours that are now second nature to myself and others who have most of their work interactions online. I have unpacked some advice I give during training and consulting when helping organisations transition to an 'office-optional' approach. And I have to admit, that during the two-year writing process, I have changed my mind as to how online meetings should be run.

I have no doubt that I will continue to learn how to make meetings matter in the online space. Lots more helpful content is available online – if you wish to continue improving your meetings and leadership practice, join me over at: onlinemeetingsthatmatter.com.

In discussing the book with people who also specialise in online team communication, I have also come to realise how culture-specific this book is. It will suit those organisations where employees are comfortable sharing their values and personal opinions, and where traditional hierarchies are breaking down or non-existent.

I hope this is you, and that this book will make the case for online meetings to become an essential part of your team's work.

Pilar Orti
London, February 2020

Introduction

YOUR BEST ONLINE MEETINGS

Let's face it, you probably have a good idea of what makes meetings matter. There is no single way of running meetings, whether they are being held online or 'in the flesh'.

I hope that you agree that a technologically glitch-free meeting that generates outcomes or strengthens our team relationships is something worth striving for; but within that, what a great meeting looks and feels like will differ between people. It might be one full of laughter, or it might be slow-paced because of an honest discussion that turns your whole project around. Maybe all you need to leave a meeting with a wide smile on your face is reassurance that you are on the right track, and have the support of your team.

I am sure that at some point you have had a great online meeting. (And if you haven't experienced online meetings yet, think of a colocated one. You'll find that some behaviours and processes can be transferred online.)

- What contributed to its success?
- What set-up did you have?
- What structure?
- What behaviours did you observe?
- What kind of preparation did you do, if any?

Different people want different things from their meetings, so before I guide you through what makes a meeting matter, here is a series of questions to help you identify what bits of guidance to follow from this book.

More importantly, answering these questions will help you pull out the knowledge you already hold within you, and help you seek out what you don't already know.

Fill in the blanks: *During our best meeting…*

I know that's a huge task. Let's break it down.

WHEN YOU LEAD A MEETING

Think of those meetings that leave you feeling like your team is on top of the world.

1. Did you and your team members do any preparation? If so, what did it consist of?

This is not a leading question. Some meetings can go really well, even if we haven't prepared for them. In fact, sometimes they go better, because instead of strictly following our plan, we listen more closely to what is going on, and adapt the meeting accordingly.

2. What structure did the meeting follow?
3. What helped the conversation flow?
4. How did people communicate agreement or disagreement, when they weren't the ones speaking?
5. How did people signal that they wanted to speak, or that they were done speaking?
6. How did you use technology to minimise disruptions to the meeting?
7. How did you end the meeting?
8. What were the outcomes of the meeting?
9. What role did you take in the meeting – were you heavily involved in the discussion? Did you play a facilitative role, or orchestrate the conversation? Did you only provide information when you were specifically asked?
10. What else did you do in the meeting – for example, did you take notes? Were you standing at your desk? Where were you located? What else was happening around you?

WHEN YOU ATTEND A MEETING

How we experience a meeting can depend on what role we take in it. You will have a different experience if you are leading a meeting, than if you are not. Besides continuously reviewing your meeting process with your team, it is worth reflecting on what *you* need when you attend a meeting that someone else is leading.

Think about a meeting you attended, or ran with people other than your team members, that went well for you.

1. Did you have time to prepare and, if so, what kind of information did you have in advance? (And how far in advance?)
2. What did the person or people running the meeting do to made you feel like you were spending your time wisely or productively?
3. With this other type of meeting in mind, think through questions 2–10 above.

Your answers to these questions will be different, when you are assuming that you are leading the meetings, to when you are not. They can help you understand your own preferences, and remind you of the experience that you want to create for team members.

MAKE YOUR MEETINGS MATTER

Keep your answers to the above questions handy. Throughout the book, some of your hunches will be challenged and others affirmed – and you will be inspired to try out a few new things.

PART 1

YOUR ECOSYSTEM

Introduction

Meetings are not the only place where your team members come together. They are one important part of your communication ecosystem, but they don't exist in isolation to the rest of your interactions online.

This section of the book will suggest what your communication ecosystem should include to make the most of your meetings. We'll look at how what happens in your meetings affects what happens outside of them.

It also will cover who should attend meetings, how frequently you should meet, and how to use a 'meeting charter' to agree on your meeting behaviours.

1

Collaboration doesn't just happen in meetings

We can think of online collaboration as having three components:

- Asynchronous gatherings – this happens in collaboration platforms such as Slack, where we post text or audio messages, knowing we will receive replies later.
- Meeting in the work – certain tasks require us to co-create a document in the cloud; we can find ourselves logged in at the same time as our collaborators.
- Real-time conversations – which happen in meetings or over chat (NB: it is best to stay away from chat for long conversations) (Figure 1).

I have heard people talk about 'collaboration' as something that only happens when we are talking in real time. But collaboration also includes working on your own towards a bigger piece – and it can suffer because individuals don't fulfil their responsibilities, not because meetings don't go well.

Figure 1: The three dimensions of collaboration

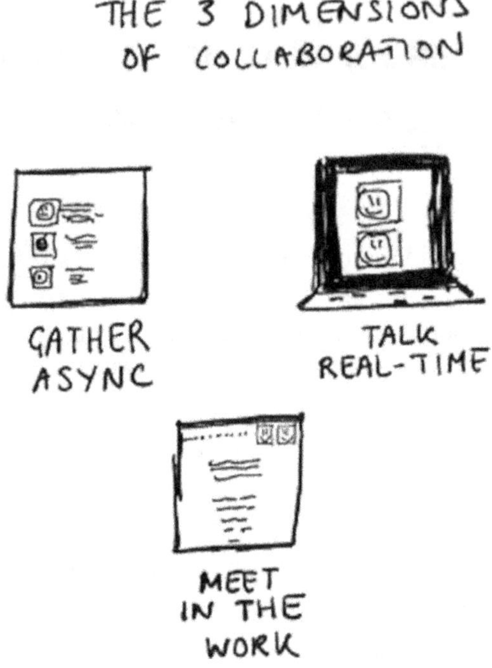

As you can see, meetings are one of the many online spaces where collaboration takes place. You should never feel like your work can't advance until your next meeting – unless you need to have a difficult conversation or discuss a complex problem. If meetings are the only time when you feel like your work as a team progresses, you are in trouble (or at least you are not taking full advantage of working online).

ASYNCHRONOUS COMMUNICATION

There was a time (not that long ago) when virtual team members communicated by phone, email and those ugly-looking spider phones which sat in the middle of the conference table and took all our focus. Meetings were the only places where we exchanged information, reported progress and made decisions.

Nowadays, there are many online tools to help us get the work done together, regardless of where we are located. All of these have a role to play in team communication:

- Collaboration platforms – where we can communicate both synchronously and asynchronously
- Project management tools – which make it easy to visualise workflow and progress (and email)[6]
- Chat tools such as Slack or Microsoft Teams – these can be used as asynchronous spaces, even if they were designed for near-real-time text conversations.

Online meetings on their own won't help you to get the work done. They are one more tool in your team's kit.

YOUR ONLINE ECOSYSTEM

When considering how to run your meetings, how often you should meet and what kinds of meetings benefit you the most, also consider the other components of your team's ecosystem. Attending meetings should feel like an integral part of your workflow and team process, rather than a disruption.

Before you think about how to run your meetings, let's quickly review your team's communication methods.

1. How do you communicate **progress** on individual tasks?
2. How do you share your **thinking** process while preparing a complex piece of work?
3. How do you make **decisions** in the team?
4. Where do you hold '**corridor conversations**' or 'water cooler chats' – those spontaneous conversations that are more helpful than formal meetings? (Figure 2)

---

6   I'm a great advocate for restricting the use of email to communication with people outside of your team, and even outside of your organisation; but some will disagree.

Figure 2: Examples of visible teamwork

If the answer to these four questions is 'in a meeting', most likely you are suffering from meeting overload. Distributed teams tend to do the above through a mixture of both synchronous and asynchronous communication, and written, audio, video and even colocated interactions. How you design your ecosystem will depend on your team's rhythm (that is, how fast you need to complete your work), your workflow and the team's make-up.

If you feel like you are meeting too frequently or that meetings are too long, consider having some of the conversations that take place in meetings in other parts of your ecosystem. Here are some examples of visible teamwork online, and some online tools that enable you to communicate asynchronously.

Communicating progress on individual tasks

Progress can be reported as it happens: for example, by using Kanban-style[7] tools, or simple spreadsheets to share which tasks you are 'Doing', and which are 'Done'.

My favourite tool for doing this is Trello. If you are using Office365, have a look at Planner. The 'To-Do' area in Basecamp works well for this, too. You can also report regularly on your tasks via iDoneThis.

Sharing your thinking process

Some teams use collaboration platforms or internal blogs to share the information and reflection that goes into substantial pieces of work that take a long time to be completed. This makes your thinking visible.

Platforms such as Slack have an option to create longer posts without taking up the whole of the discussion space. You could consider creating a group blog on a blogging platform such as Wordpress; or for sensitive information, create a folder in your online team space for text documents.

Making decisions in the team

Instead of circulating documents with the aim of discussing them in the meeting, you can use editable documents to gather input into complex decisions. Google Docs and Office365 enable you to comment on documents. Microsoft Teams also enables you to have a conversation around a document.

Holding 'corridor conversations' or 'water cooler chats'

Some teams and organisations have dedicated areas in their collaboration platforms dedicated to random and non-work-related, text-based conversations. Slack, Microsoft Teams and Basecamp all allow you to create areas dedicated to 'random chat' (or however you want to name them).

---

7   A Kanban board allows you to visualise the progress of the different steps in a project (see Chapter 22).

. . . .

INSPIRATION

Automattic is the company behind the blogging platform Wordpress. At the time of writing, it has more than 1,200 employees distributed around the world, with no company offices.1 As asynchronous communication is the most efficient way of communicating across time zones, employees communicate complex thoughts in writing. They also use chat, video meetings, audio and in-person retreats, but their main collaboration channel is the written form.

On the other hand, at Meet Edgar (the company behind the social media scheduling tool of the same name), employees need to be available for synchronous conversation on instant messaging, or audio or video calls, throughout their working day. For that reason, the company only recruits those working in American time zones.[8]

. . . .

MAKE YOUR MEETINGS MATTER

- Think about what happens in your meetings. Can any of these conversations be moved to an asynchronous space to make room for better conversations during meetings?
- At your next meeting, think through the conversations. Was it necessary to have this particular conversation in real time? Was then the best time to have it?
- How do your other communication channels integrate or complement your meetings?

---

8 You can find out more about Meet Edgar in Virtual Not Distant (2018) 'WLP 152: Clarity and Transparency at Meet Edgar', podcast. Available at: www.virtualnotdistant.com/podcasts/meet-edgar

2

The effect of meetings on teamwork

Just as meetings can be affected by other team processes, meeting behaviours will influence how the team operates beyond them. Meetings can give rise to norms (unwritten rules) that spread into other areas of our work.

It's worth paying attention not only to how productive your meetings are, but also to the behaviours that emerge during them, and those that you role-model as a manager.

As meetings are the only time in which team members have high-bandwidth, real-time conversations, team norms are more likely to emerge in the online space than they would if team members were to regularly converse outside them, as happens in the colocated office.

Let's illustrate this with a couple of scenarios (Table 1).

Table 1: Negative types of team norm

Team norm	In-meeting behaviour	Beyond the meeting
Meetings belong to the manager	The manager always does most of the talking, reporting on progress, delegating tasks and telling everyone what to do.	Team members show little initiative to problem-solve or innovate in their day-to-day work. They only do the work they have been assigned, as opposed to actively helping others or looking for ways to improve how the team operates. They expect the manager to take the lead in improving team processes.

Everyone has something to say about everything	As the meeting gets going, everyone comments and has a say on everyone else's work, regardless of whether they are directly involved in the task or project.	People start to feel reluctant to share their work and progress in public, for fear that they will be criticised or have to defend their course of action. Or team members become so heavily dependent on each other that they reach out to other team members every time they have to make a decision, however small.
Conflicts are left unresolved	Conflicts and important disagreements arise at meetings, but they are left unresolved until they can be tackled at the next meeting (and the next, and so on). Team members leave the meetings frustrated and unable to get on with their work.	The absence of conflict resolution at meetings means that team members aren't clear about the direction in which to take their work. They feel unable to continue disagreeing outside of the meeting, as it was decided to resolve differences at the next meeting. Eventually, no one bothers to disagree with anyone else, and problems are not flagged up.

Let's now balance these less-than-ideal scenarios with more positive ones (Table 2).

Table 2: Positive types of team norm

Team norm	In-meeting behaviour	Beyond the meeting
Meetings belong to the team	The manager adopts the role of 'facilitator',* asking team members to report on their own work. The manager only takes part in the conversation when there is something specific to contribute.	Team members feel ownership of the team process and their work. When they come across a problem, they try to address it on their own, or by reaching out to the person best suited to help them, instead of always asking the manager for help.
Conversations are not restricted to meetings	When issues aren't resolved at a meeting (for example, conflict is unresolved or a decision isn't made), those involved agree on how they will continue the discussion after the meeting is over.	Team members get used to conversing asynchronously or in small groups. They tackle disagreements as they come up, instead of waiting to resolve them at the next team meeting.

*A professional facilitator helps team members achieve a common objective in a meeting. They need not be subject experts, and they take a neutral stance. As a manager you won't be neutral, and you might be a subject expert – but by adopting a facilitator's mindset, you can assist team members to make and own their decisions, rather than buying into, or building on, those you make yourself.

These examples illustrate how meeting behaviours can spread to other areas of teamwork (Figure 3). In a similar way, some problems we see in meetings reflect that something is wrong in other areas of our work or communication.

**Figure 3: Behaviours in your meetings can
spread to other areas of teamwork**

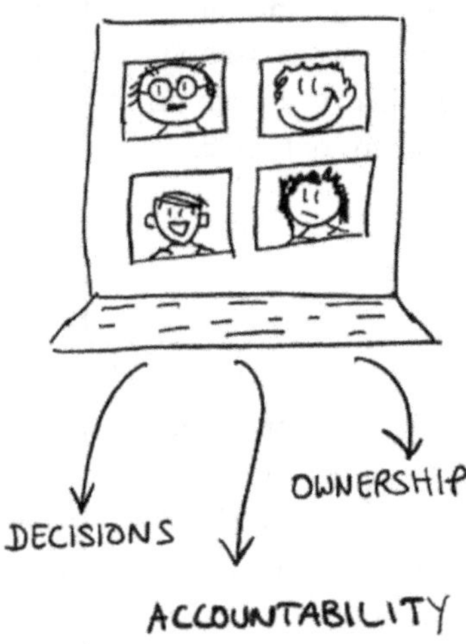

In Chapter 3 we'll look at some common 'meeting symptoms' and how you can cure them. But before we do that, let's continue looking at how meetings can be integrated into your wider communication ecosystem.

YOUR MEETINGS MICROSYSTEM

In addition to your broader communications ecosystem, you will need to build a 'microsystem' around your meetings. This can include the following.

A dedicated space online for meetings and documentation

This can be a group or channel in your collaboration platform, or a folder in your storage space to keep your agendas or points of conversation, any information you need to share before or during the meeting and meeting notes.

Visible and editable agendas or points of conversation

We will come back to agendas in Chapter 22. For now, let's think about where you will create and share agendas for those meetings that require them, as well as where you will take and store notes from your meetings.

Templates to run regular meetings

If you run the same type of meeting regularly, create a template[9] so that you don't have to reinvent the wheel every time you meet. As well as saving time, a template should enable anyone in the team to run a meeting.

An online area where you can follow up conversations or actions that emerge during meetings

Sometimes we need to end a meeting before the conversation is over. Sometimes we realise that the piece of information we want to pass on is not at our fingertips, and it might take five minutes for us to dig it out. Or there might be relevant thoughts that come to us as soon as we leave the meeting.

For these reasons, it's worth having an asynchronous space where you can continue conversations after everyone has logged off. This could be in the form of comments or notes in your editable agenda, or in the dedicated space for meetings and documentation.

Keep directions to the 'room' handy

Most online meetings take place via a URL. If your meeting software allows you to mark a meeting as recurrent, keeping the URL handy in a pinned post or in the channel description in your collaboration space will save everyone time. Or you can create a recurring meeting for the team, which includes the relevant URL and can be easily added to people's calendars.

---

9   You can find a collection of templates over at www.lucidmeetings.com. Even though most of them have been created with colocated meetings in mind, they are easy to adapt.

MAKE YOUR MEETINGS MATTER

- If meetings are essential to your work and need to be regular, review your communication ecosystem. Is it easy to find information on them? To find the action points?
- What norms have developed during your team meetings? Is there anything you would like to change or reinforce?
- Go through the list of team norms and consider how they are reflected in in-meeting and beyond-the-meeting behaviour. Are any of these norms present in your team? Are there other behaviours you see reflected somewhere else that you would like to change?

3

Your meeting schedule

Between the 1960s and 2017, scheduled, colocated meetings involving executives increased in length and frequency from ten weekly hours to 23.[10] Meetings can gradually munch away at people's time, leaving many to make up for lost hours by going into work early, staying late or working over weekends.[11] In the online space – and especially if team members are working from home – there is an even greater danger of people overworking. On top of that, meetings that are run badly can lead to an aversion to meetings in general: a common phenomenon in today's organisations.

Meetings shouldn't be a necessary evil; they should be a part of how we get certain aspects of our work done. But whereas we can expect some meetings to be less than fruitful (just as we have days when we get little work done), we should never expect meetings to be irrelevant or a waste of time.

Before you decide when and how you will hold your meetings, think about whether they are necessary. Don't meet regularly online by default, or because you've heard it's common practice among virtual teams. *Meet because you want to achieve something together.*

For example, if your tasks are interdependent and synchronous conversation is the quickest and most effective way of checking in, it might be useful to have daily meetings.

Conversely, if people regularly communicate asynchronously and there is a culture of picking up the phone or hopping on a video call when necessary, a monthly meeting might be all that you need. Even though

---

10   Leslie A. Perlow, Constance Noonan Hadley and Eunice Eun (2017) 'Stop the meeting madness: How to free up time for meaningful work'. *Harvard Business Review* 95(4): 62–69.

11   Gartner (2017) 'Remote workers tend to work longer hours, UK Study finds', 11 October. Available at: www.cebglobal.com/talentdaily/remote-workers-tend-to-work-longer-hours-uk-study-finds/

the whole team meets only once a month, communication will still flow through your other channels.

When considering how often to schedule team meetings, ask yourself this question:

- What are our team meetings for?

Break this down as much as you can. If you have different types of meetings, analyse each of them.

- How much communication flows between team members day-to-day?
- How do we update each other on our work?
- How does collaboration happen in our team?

Answering the above questions might be particularly important if your team is transitioning from being colocated to remote, or if the nature of your work has changed.

You will need to reconsider how, when and why you hold your meetings. For example, if you have just gone through a fast-paced period, your daily meetings will have been key to keeping your work aligned; however, when you move on to a project with a slower tempo, you might find that meeting once a week is enough.

YOUR MEETING RHYTHM

Once you get into some sort of meeting rhythm, look out for signs such as the ones below which can tell you that the cadence of your meetings is not right, and that you need to adjust your schedule.

Table 3: How to solve meeting rhythm issues

Problem	Solution
You can't keep up with the text-based communication, resulting in miscommunication and misalignment (and stressing everyone out).	You probably should meet more often. Meetings can help reduce the amount of asynchronous communication, and promote better understanding between everyone.
Team members are getting their own work done at odd hours, because their official work time is being taken up by meetings.	You're meeting way too often.
The only thing your team members say during the meeting is: "Nothing to update you on, same as usual."	Guess what? You're meeting too often.
Your meetings last 2½ hours and you're all so exhausted after them that you can't do any more work.	Consider chunking up the meetings and meeting more regularly, but for shorter periods of time. Or consider meeting in smaller groups.
The conversations on your online platforms seem to go on and on, with comments such as: "I don't think you quite understood me there? What I meant was…" "I thought we had agreed on…"	It's probably time to set a more regular meeting rhythm, to help with your communication. Alternatively, encourage people to jump on a call if a thread is getting long and convoluted.
Your meetings are optional, and the number of participants is starting to decrease.	It's time to review your meeting schedule, the nature of your meetings and the workflow in your team. Dig deeper to see whether this reflects a general lack of interest in other team members and the work. Think of holding fewer meetings, and make them more focused.

Warning!

You and your team members might be having so much fun together that you become 'meeting junkies'. Maybe you find yourselves organising meetings every time something new pops up, or to make small decisions that could be made by an individual without everyone else's involvement.

Being in a meeting can energise us as we make plans, discuss options and imagine a better future together. When we get on with our team members, spending time with them releases hormones that make us feel good.[12] These conversations can be key to our work, but we also have to make sure that we then pursue those action plans that we have committed to in the meeting.

If your days get longer and longer because you're spending a lot of time in animated conversation, it might be time to cut down on meetings, however rewarding they are.

KEEP MEETINGS AS SHORT AS THEY NEED TO BE

It's OK to meet for 15 minutes. It doesn't matter if the meeting was scheduled for an hour and is cut short – remember, no one had to travel from the other end of town to attend. There is nothing to say that you can't end the meeting once everything has been covered. (I have been at meetings where we were stretching out the time so as not to conclude before the scheduled finishing time. That's crazy!)

When organising your meetings, schedule them in a way that suits you best, not in the way your scheduling tools allow you. Jason Fried brings this up beautifully in the book *ReWork*:

> Meetings are typically scheduled like TV shows. You set aside thirty minutes or an hour because that's how scheduling software works (you'll never see anyone schedule a seven-minute meeting with Outlook). Too bad. If it only takes seven minutes to accomplish

---

12   More data to support this statement is necessary, but I came across a study that confirms the release of the bonding hormone oxytocin during social media browsing and interactions. If that is the case, thinking that we release oxytocin during online real-time interactions doesn't seem too far off. Adam L. Penenberg (2010) 'Social networking affects brains like falling in love', *Fast Company*, 1 July. Available at: www.fastcompany.com/1659062/social-networking-affects-brains-falling-love

a meeting's goal, then that's all the time you should spend. Don't stretch seven into thirty.[13]

Scheduling meetings in this way is probably a hangover from when we needed to book meeting rooms in office buildings. This is one added advantage of holding meetings online: we don't need to do that, so meetings can be as long or as short as they need to be.

ARE YOU 'GIGGING IT' OR 'JAMMING IT'?

Sometimes it is suitable to think of meetings as 'gigs' or 'jams'.[14] At Infinite Red, a company that designs and develops apps, employees communicate what kind of meeting is being called, to make sure that everyone is aware of how it will be run.

Gigs are traditional, well-run meetings:

- With an agenda (if no agenda is ready, the meeting is cancelled)
- With a designated host – a person who will run the meeting
- They start and end as planned
- They have follow-up notes
- Tangents and distractions are not allowed

Jams are more relaxed meetings:

- They are places for 'experimentation, exploration and finding new frontiers'[15]
- The meeting schedule is loose, and attendance is not mandatory
- Even attention itself is not mandatory.

---

13   Jason Fried (2010) *ReWork: Change the Way You Work Forever*, Ebury Publishing (Kindle Edition), locations 719–722.

14   Gigs are performance events with a set programme; in jams, performers improvise as the event progresses.

15   Gant Laborde (2018) 'Virtual meetings have types', Infinite Red, 29 March. Available at: https://shift.infinite.red/virtual-meetings-have-types-4a13b3744639

This means that if you want to make sure a person is involved at a certain point in the discussion, you have to 'activate' them. For example, imagine you are debating whether to change the look of your website, and you want Rachel to take part in the discussion. (Rachel is great, she always comes up with creative solutions.)

You say, "Rachel, what do you think of this suggestion?" If Rachel is doing something else online at that point, that's all right. You just bring her up to speed, and she can give you her opinion. With no strict agendas or hard stops, a team can give an issue the time that it needs to be discussed in depth during a jam.

In his article explaining the difference between a gig and a jam, Gant Laborde, Chief Technology Strategist at Infinite Red, emphasises the importance of determining whether a meeting will be a gig or a jam when a meeting is called. This helps align everyone's expectations about what the meeting will achieve and, as mentioned above, how it will be run. At Infinite Red, they refer people to that article as part of the onboarding system, although it is using the terms 'gig' and 'jam' in actual conversation that makes it effective.

MAKE YOUR MEETINGS MATTER

- Is your meeting rhythm right for your team's communication patterns?
- If meetings feel too long, are there any communication systems that could help slim down the agenda? Use Table 3 to identify any signs that the cadence of your meetings is not right.
- If you think your meeting schedule is optimal, check with your team members – they might have a different idea.

4

Creating a 'meeting charter'

Creating a 'meeting charter' helps a team to be involved in setting the cadence of meetings, making discussions more effective and setting expectations of involvement. This live document (to be updated as your team evolves, or the nature of your work changes) can assist with onboarding new members to your team.

Here is a list of questions to help you create your document (you will notice that we have covered some in the previous chapters): remember to review it periodically. Some of these practices will emerge organically as you run more meetings. If that is the case, you can use this list of questions to help you review your current meeting habits, and decide whether there is anything you would like to change.

FREQUENCY

- How frequently shall we gather together to:
  - Review our team process?
  - Talk through our work progress?
  - Review our meetings?
  - Celebrate?
- Which of our meetings are optional? (For inspiration, refer to Chapter 3 on gigs and jams.)

BEFORE THE MEETING

- How will the agenda or meeting content be created (when needed)?
- How will prep work (when needed) be communicated?
- Where shall we gather the information we need before the meeting starts?

- What are our expectations about how people turn up to meetings? For example, attending meetings from a quiet space, muted microphones when there is background noise, camera levelled to see faces comfortably, etc.

DURING THE MEETING

- How shall we decide who starts and ends the meeting?
- If we need to take notes, how shall we gather them online while we run the meeting? What tools do we need?
- Where can we follow up on our discussions asynchronously?
- How shall we make decisions? Will we agree on this before the meeting, or during it?

COMMUNICATION

- How often shall we use video?
- What shall we use as a backchannel, in case we have problems with the tech?
- What visual signs or words in the chat shall we use during conversation?

For example, some meeting platforms have built-in icons or emojis which can be used to communicate. Agree on those you would like to use, and what each of them mean. You can come up with your own written vocabulary, too (see the 'Inspiration' box below).

BEYOND OUR CURRENT TEAM

- What do we need new team members to know about our meetings?
- How and when should we invite those outside our team to our meetings?

· ·

INSPIRATION

The members of Transition Network1[16] have a code to communicate in the chat box, when they are not on video. These written abbreviations can be adapted to when you are in front of the webcam, and want to contribute to the conversation with a short intervention.

> h = Hand up. "I would like to speak."
> hh = Two hands. 'I have additional information to what the current speaker is saying.'
> A = Quick feedback to speaker: "Sounds good", or "I agree".
> W = Silent applause, celebration.
> T = "I would like to make a technical point."
> L = Language. "I don't understand."
> Q = "I have a question."
> y = Yes
> n = No

· ·

MAKE YOUR MEETINGS MATTER

- If you are a new team, review how happy you are with how your meetings are going regularly – for example, every third meeting.
- Use the meeting charter to help you have the conversation.

---

16   Nenad Maljković (2016) 'Virtual team quick guide', Medium.com, 6 August. Available at: https://medium.com/virtual-teams-for-systemic-change/virtual-team-quick-guide-95736861e4ab

5

Your ecosystem wrap-up

As you can see, how you run your meetings can have quite an effect on the rest of your teamwork. Meetings have become an integral part of work life, leading to research on how they affect job satisfaction. There is some evidence that 'employees who view their meetings as satisfying and effective tend to be more satisfied with their jobs in general'.[17] It's worth paying attention to how we run our meetings, and the part they play in our overall team process.

Here are some actions you can take following what we have covered in Part 1.

- **Take time to pull your experience of good meetings together.** You are bound to know quite a bit about running a good online meeting from past experience already, or from attending them.
- **Review your team's collaboration ecosystem.** Could it be better integrated into your meeting schedule? Are you relying too much on meetings for progress or non-complex information?
- **Observe the behaviours in your meetings.** Are any of them mirrored in how people collaborate or approach their work?
- **Ask yourself: do our meetings get in the way of other work?** Or is there miscommunication and lack of alignment because we don't meet often enough? With the help of the meeting charter, review how frequently you meet, and how your meetings are run.

---

17 Joseph E. Mroz and Joseph Andrew Allen (2015) 'It's all in how you use it: Managers' use of meetings to reduce employee intentions to quit'. *Consulting Psychology Journal Practice and Research* 67(4): 348–361, p. 349. Available at: www.researchgate.net/publication/287107772_ It%27S_all_in_how_you_use_it_Managers%27_use_of_meetings_to_reduce_employee_ intentions_to_quit

PART 2

RELATIONSHIPS

Introduction

Every time we interact with someone else, our relationship with them is affected. Every email, phone call and video conversation can affect how we see others and what they feel about us.

There has been little acknowledgement of this in the business world, where anything to do with emotions seems to be left outside the office. And as colocated meetings rarely aim to strengthen our relationships, sometimes we forget that *how* we interact with each other matters. We can become so intent on getting through our agenda (after all, "This is a work meeting!") that in rushing through some off-topic conversations, we don't see how we might be undervaluing a team member's contribution. Or we don't see the value of spending half an hour discussing our strategy, which might be just what one of our team members needs to feel connected to the team's purpose.

This section, which focuses on nurturing the relationships in your team, will go beyond suggesting that you hold social meetings or set aside time to hold non-work conversations. It will focus mainly on how to build trust and strengthen work relationships through your meetings.

<u>6</u>

Not engagement,
but ownership

Deci and Ryan's self-determination theory (Figure 4) suggests that we are all driven to behave in effective and healthy ways as long as we feel a sense of autonomy, competence and relatedness.[18] Therefore, the role of managers is not to 'motivate' people, but to create an environment for intrinsic motivation to emerge. This is no different in the online space.

Figure 4: Self-determination theory

---

18   You can find out more about the theory from the dedicated website http://selfdeterminationtheory.org/. I also recommend Daniel Pink's book, *Drive*, which is full of research on motivation. He adapted Deci and Ryan's theory, keeping 'autonomy' as a component, but replacing 'competence' with 'mastery', and 'relatedness' with 'purpose'. Daniel Pink (2018) *Drive: The Surprising Truth About What Motivates Us*, Canongate Books.

We can:

- Have **autonomy** via access to the tools and people we need to work with, without having to be at our company's offices.
- Remain **competent** by quickly accessing the information we need to do our work, and learning 'on demand'.
- Fulfil our need to **connect with others** by pressing a button that says 'Like'.

This is why a manager can't be solely responsible for the success of team meetings. It's time to design processes and systems that enable all team members to be equally involved and responsible for running meetings well.

RELEVANCE AS AN ANTIDOTE TO MULTITASKING

I was attending a networking event in a cosy London café. It was an informal set-up, with only a few of us round the table.

When I mentioned that my job was to help people work in remote teams, the subject of online meetings came up.

"Ah yes," said one of the other attendees. "We are a remote team and we've made using video compulsory. That way people don't get distracted by other stuff because they are visible on video constantly, and they have no choice but to focus."

That is an easy way to decrease someone's sense of autonomy. It's also an example of treating a symptom without understanding the cause. If you are worried about people checking their email or browsing the internet during team meetings, it's better to find out why they are distracting themselves, rather than controlling their behaviour by forcing them to turn on their video.

If team members are focusing on unrelated activities during meetings, it could mean that they feel they have little to contribute to, or gain from, them. It could reflect how they are feeling about the team's work. Your reason for using video should be to enhance quality of conversation, rather than to strong-arm team members into paying attention.

At the same time, if a team member suddenly remembers in the middle of a meeting that they need to reply to an email and can't get it off their mind, the best thing they can do to stay engaged is to write the message and forget about it. If they want to do the gardening during an audio call, why not? In colocated meetings, people will doodle, take notes, their minds might wander off, they might look out of a window to rest their eyes. When online, some people might need to distract themselves now and then to remain engaged.

Suggesting a vocabulary for people – even when they are not speaking – is one way to help them stay involved in the conversation. On video this is easily done by encouraging people to use hand signals or gestures to show their reactions when others are speaking, or by holding up pieces of paper with simple drawings.

MAGNIFIED BEHAVIOURS

The above behaviours become a problem when they distract the person carrying them out, or when they distract someone else, which can easily happen when we are on video. In that case, it's fair to ask team members to be fully present at the meeting, or switch their webcam off while they finish that niggling task, or mute themselves while they are typing away.

If the only experience that some team members have had of attending online meetings is webinars (which are not meetings, but presentations), or they have only experienced a broadcast approach to online gatherings, you will need to let them know that they are expected to take an active part in the conversation online.

MIX AND MATCH

People find some types of meetings easier to contribute to than others. For example, you might enjoy status updates because they are structured and predictable, whereas Rachel, one of your team members, much prefers strategic meetings because responding to other people's ideas helps her formulate her own.

For this reason, it's worth holding different types of meetings to increase the chances of people getting value out of discussing the work in the company of others, and of contributing to meetings as fully as they can. If you hold all your meetings in the same way – for example, by having a prepared, rigid agenda – you might be limiting how team members contribute to them.

We don't always know what we enjoy (or what bores us) until we experience it. If we limit our experience to those meetings with a tight agenda, we might never discover that we thrive in an environment where we can discuss and analyse one aspect of our work in an unstructured way. Holding all meetings in the same way could prevent team members from discovering an alternative method of communicating that suits their personalities and communication styles better.

NOTHING'S PERFECT

Remember the good old days, when we had to deal with bad sound-proofing in meeting rooms, broken heaters in the middle of winter and double-booked rooms?

The online spaces where we meet are bound to bring problems with them too, and these affect how engaged people are in meetings. Be prepared for problems with bandwidth and servers, and for having to use platforms with unattractive interfaces. There will always be things that get in the way of great meetings (how to overcome these is covered in in Part 4).

MAKE YOUR MEETINGS MATTER

- Think about how you run meetings. Do you think team members experience a sense of autonomy, competence or relatedness? Are some meetings more likely to achieve this?
- How do you decide how to run meetings? Ask team members how they prefer to contribute to them.

7

A question of trust

When we find commonalities in different areas of our lives, we feel more connected to others. This can lead to feeling more comfortable sharing our doubts and problems with them, because we think they are like us: familiarity helps us feel safe.

Trust emerges when we understand other people's behaviours, especially if their thinking patterns are different to our own. Trust emerges when we understand the values that drive people's decisions, and we realise that they are trying to do the right thing – even if their 'right thing' looks different to ours.

Team meetings are a good place to build trust, because we can have real-time conversations in which to ask someone to clarify their process or the reasoning behind their comments and decisions. When we talk to others, we can swiftly go into detail about the thinking behind our actions, instead of spending half an hour rewriting a message to make sure that it can't be misinterpreted. Even those team members not directly involved in a discussion can benefit from hearing how we talk about our work, and how our values drive the decisions we make.

Online meetings don't just provide us with information that moves our work forward; they give us information about our colleagues that otherwise we wouldn't pick up.

When you think about how to run your meetings, consider the level of trust that exists in the team. For example, do people in the team own up to mistakes? If they do, it's probably a sign that they trust that no one will hold it against them: to admit to a mistake, you need to feel that no one will think you messed up on purpose, or because of carelessness.

TRUST EMERGES IN DIFFERENT WAYS

In her book *The Culture Map*, Erin Meyer suggests that there are two types of trust, cognitive and affective: Cognitive trust is based on 'the confidence you feel in another person's accomplishments, skills, and reliability', while affective trust 'arises from feelings of emotional closeness, empathy, or friendship'[19] (Figure 5).

Your own tendency might be to focus on whether others fulfil their offer of help, deliver their work on time, and their work is of high quality. Or maybe you look for a more personal way of connecting with another person, and find this easier to do during real-time conversations.

Getting to know each other well requires having a mental image of the person, hearing their voice, seeing their facial expressions. Technology can help us achieve this.

Figure 5: Cognitive and affective trust

19　Erin Meyer (2016) *The Culture Map: Decoding How People Think, Lead, and Get Things Done Across Cultures*, PublicAffairs (Kindle Edition), location 2428.

TRUST, AUDIO AND VIDEO

Using video for meetings has been widely adopted in remote teams, especially in start-ups and small businesses. While teams that still are using the company's offices as a base prefer to hold colocated team meetings, teams that are 100% virtual have embraced video.

This doesn't mean that all teams will benefit from using video all of the time, but it is worth considering how and when it can benefit your team. Webcams can improve communication by bringing gestures and facial expressions into the mix, as well as help to keep the conversation fluid, as team members can better judge when to intervene in a conversation. It's easier to look out for visual cues signalling that someone wants to continue speaking, than it is to infer it over audio.

Seeing each other's faces also reminds us (consciously or subconsciously) that we are human: that we have feelings, not just thoughts. In this way, we can be kinder to each other.

. . . .

I experienced an example of this not too long ago. I was running a session for an online community, and had let initial introductions go off on a tangent and ramble on a bit. The participants were still getting used to hearing each other speak. One of my friends present as a participant thought that I was losing control of the session, and interrupted the conversation to enthusiastically "move us along".

That stung. Not only had she publicly shown that she thought I needed help to facilitate the conversation, but she had interrupted a valuable exercise. Being careful not to confront her in front of everyone else, I said something to diffuse her comment, and everyone continued introducing themselves.

I muted myself and typed a private message in the chat box, asking my friend not to do that again, and to trust that I knew what I was doing. I watched her as she received the message: her expression changed as she read it – the joy and excitement at being at the event disappeared from her face.

I realised then that she hadn't meant to undermine me. She started typing in the chat, apologising, saying it was a terrible habit of hers that she was working on stopping. Looking at her gutted expression, I knew she had simply made a mistake.

My next message to her was "Don't worry about it", and we were able to move on. Seeing her face as she received my message prompted me to react in the best interest of our relationship. Had it been an audio-only conversation, her silence would have been open to interpretation and I might have damaged our relationship.

. . . .

SHOULD WE TALK ABOUT THE WEATHER?

If you turn to the internet for guidance on how to lead a remote team, you will come across plenty of advice suggesting that you put aside time for non-work-related conversation during meetings, creating the opportunity to 'check in as people'. This makes sense when you know that affective trust is built in this way.

Some teams run short icebreakers at the start of a meeting (such as sharing their favourite foods, or something they have been up to lately), and some teams might go as far as to banning 'business talk' for the first few minutes of their meetings. Some teams hold regular 'happy hours', while others hold 'virtual coffees' to provide space for colleagues to have non-work-related conversations. So far, I have not come across any research finding that those kinds of practices or activities lead to better results or more trusting relationships; but I also have not come across any research to say that they can damage your team.

Again, you will need to judge how much time you should set aside for non-work conversations, and whether you want to hold meetings solely for social chat. 'Virtual coffees' will be covered in Chapter 16, so for now, let's assess how much time you should set aside for small talk in your meetings, and think about how sociable your team is as a whole.

Do you enjoy each other's company?

If you find each other's company enjoyable, how about kicking off the meeting with a round of personal catch-ups, or using other random questions (see 'Generating social chatter' below) to end meetings and celebrate the fact that you all get along? Alternatively, if you are a team that doesn't enjoy socialising, a quick check-in at the beginning of the meeting will be sufficient.

Do you prefer to separate work and life?[20]

Some people prefer to keep their work life separate from their personal life. They might enjoy their colleagues' company, but don't want to give away much about their existence outside work. In that case, a question such as "Is there anything going on at your end we should know about?" might be appropriate and sufficient to kick off a meeting.

Do you stay in touch through asynchronous communication every day?

If you do, perhaps you are already caught up with small talk and don't need to make room for it in every meeting.

Do you work together on tasks and regularly hop on a call when you need help?

On the one hand, if your team members are in touch with each other frequently due of the nature of the work, your meetings probably need little small talk, as you will already know what is going on in each other's lives. On the other hand, if you meet once every two weeks or once a month and don't interact much in-between meetings, then a few minutes to reconnect as individuals in every meeting will help you remember that you are a team – not just people working in parallel towards a common goal.

THE VALUE OF SOCIAL CHAT AT THE BEGINNING OF A MEETING

Starting a meeting with a quick round of social chat helps everyone become present and feel like they are in the same space. Furthermore, making that initial effort to contribute to the conversation helps to generate more dialogue later.

---

20   I am aware that the word 'life' in phrases such as 'work–life balance' is not the most accurate one: after all, work is also a part of life. For 'non-work-related activities', I will stick to the more common term 'life'.

There is another practical side to starting a meeting with small talk: the opportunity to test everyone's sound and connectivity. It's much better to realise during a bit of preliminary chit-chat that your computer settings need to be adjusted because you have bought a new headset, rather than noticing it in the middle of an important discussion when you are expressing your views beautifully, and everyone starts shouting, "We can't hear you!"

In addition, you should double-check whether background noise is too loud for you to keep your microphone open throughout the meeting. Plus if your internet connection is dodgy, you can figure that out during the social catch-up, and adjust your speaking rhythm accordingly.

Generating social chatter

It can feel awkward to sit in front of a monitor and have a social conversation when you are not used to it. Having a structure to the conversation can make it flow. If you decide to encourage social conversations in your meetings, include these in your meeting plan or agenda, so that it doesn't feel like time is being wasted with small talk.

Here are some suggestions on how to kick off a meeting with the aim of fostering social connection. They are listed in order of degree of informality, starting with suggestions for teams where members don't know each other well, who have a strong identity as serious professionals, or where people don't like to get too personal. The last set of prompts are more likely to be embraced by teams that see themselves as 'wacky' or 'alternative'.

- Have you tried out a new tool recently? (Great for those who are always experimenting and love trying out shiny new things.)
- Anything you've read lately of particular interest? (You can get to know someone by hearing what they enjoy reading.)
- Any productivity strategies you've recently discovered? (Hey, you can kill two birds with one stone with this one!)
- Any interesting podcasts you're listening to? How about a recommended episode that might help us with our work? (This is also a good opportunity to remind people that there are ways of seeking information away from the screen.)
- Describe what's on the other side of your camera, right in

front of you, that we can't see. (This can give you an idea of the person's current physical environment.)

- Tell us what people have been up to in your part of the world lately.
- Show us a picture of your favourite food, or take a picture during the week of what you had for lunch. How often do you have that kind of food/dish?
- What time is it now where you are, and what wouldn't/shouldn't you do at that time?
- Is today very different to every other day?
- Give us a tour! (Take your teammates around your home or your workspace or office if you have a laptop, or pan your office with the webcam if you are on a workstation. If you are going to suggest this, give people working at home a bit of notice, should they want to tidy up.)[21]
- Sing us a song. What tune has been buzzing in your mind lately?

Remember that your team members will enjoy small talk in different ways and at different levels, so make sure you vary how you encourage it in your meetings.

. . . .

WHEN SMALL TALK GETS IN THE WAY

I always try to arrive at meetings a few minutes before they start. I want to make sure the tech is ready. If we are going to be looking at a document, or if I'm going to be sharing information, I like to have everything to hand.

Sometimes, someone else will have joined the meeting already and start chatting to me. I politely engage in conversation while I'm adjusting the camera, browsing the internet for the right website, or pulling up the shared document to guide us through the meeting.

. . . .

---

21   Only suggest that people share their home space if you have seen them do that comfortably and intentionally before, and if you know that team members are happy blending their personal and professional lives.

If you arrive early to a meeting, make sure you are not preventing others from settling in. Some team members log in early to prepare themselves for the meeting, but they might be too polite to tell you that your conversation is disturbing them. If in doubt, ask: "Shall I give you a few minutes while you're setting up?"

Is small talk overrated?

In the *Harvard Business Review* article, 'Small talk is an overrated way to build relationships with employees', Kim Scott suggests that instead of worrying about providing opportunities for social talk, managers should focus on giving feedback.[22] In principle, I agree with the point she is making: while we should take an interest in a person's life, informal conversations about work can help to build strong work relationships.

Having said that, let's remember that Scott's article was written predominantly with a colocated workforce in mind, where small talk can take place in the office easily, spontaneously and briefly. In the remote space, non-work-related conversation might be the fastest way of helping people feel at ease, so that they feel ready to go on to more work-focused conversations and can build affective trust.

The jury is out on this one: it really depends on what you and your team want and need.

MAKE YOUR MEETINGS MATTER

- Thinking about the two ways in which trust develops among people: have you got enough of a mix of conversations to cater for different trust-building preferences?
- Do you use video in your meetings? What are the benefits of this (either using it or not)?
- Observe how different people interact with each other, the kind of questions they ask of each other, the anecdotes and information they share. It will give you a good idea of the type of information currently being shared.

---

22   Kim Scott (2017b) 'Small talk is an overrated way to build relationships with employees'. *Harvard Business Review*, 25 July. Available at: https://hbr.org/2017/07/small-talk-is-an-overrated-way-to-build-relationships-with-your-employees

- Discuss with your team what kinds of check-ins and check-outs would help them to feel connected. Consider rotating the responsibility for running these.

8

Creating psychological safety

In a team with high psychological safety, teammates feel safe to take risks around their team members. They feel confident that no one on the team will embarrass or punish anyone else for admitting a mistake, asking a question, or offering a new idea.[23]

Although it was Amy Edmondson who first identified and studied the concept of 'psychological safety',[24] it became popular after Google shared the findings of 'Project Aristotle', launched in 2015.

As part of this project, the researchers studied team member and manager behaviour during meetings. They expected high-performance teams to share some practices, such as catching up with non-work-related matters before meetings, reviewing their work periodically or making sure that meetings were completely business-focused.

However, they only found one commonality among high-performance teams: they had developed group norms that 'created a sense of togetherness while also encouraging people to take a chance'.[25] They had developed psychological safety (Figure 6).

---

23   ReWork (nd) 'Guides: Identify dynamics of effective teams'. Available at: https://rework. withgoogle.com/guides/understanding-team-effectiveness/steps/identify-dynamics-of-effective-teams/

24   Harvard Business Review (2019) 'Creating psychological safety in the Workplace', podcast, 22 January. Available at: https://hbr.org/podcast/2019/01/creating-psychological-safety-in-the-workplace

25   Charles Duhigg (2016) *Smarter Faster Better: The Secrets of Being Productive*, Random House (Kindle Edition), location 731.

Figure 6: Psychological safety

Google's research showed that managers and leaders of these teams shared a set of behaviours. They:

- Invited people to speak up
- Talked about their own emotions
- Didn't interrupt others
- Showed it was OK to intervene when someone was concerned or upset
- Tried to anticipate how people would react, then worked to accommodate those reactions

CREATING PSYCHOLOGICAL SAFETY IN ONLINE MEETINGS

Although Google's research took place in colocated meetings, the findings are of use to working in the online space. In *Smarter, Faster, Better*, Charles Duhigg neatly summarises the project and follows it up with advice to managers running a meeting. Before we have a look at how his five recommendations can be adapted to the online space, there is another consideration uniquely related to running meetings online.

Make sure everyone is comfortable with the tech

At the time of writing, not every knowledge-worker will have taken part in an online meeting. There is also diversity in how meeting platforms look and operate. Some of them always work well, while others give us problems from time to time. Feeling comfortable in the meeting space helps us feel psychologically safe.

If you are comfortable with technology and can navigate tech challenges with a cool head, watch out: this might not be the case for other team members. Don't underestimate the anxiety of feeling helpless in the face of technological problems. (For how to make sure that everyone is comfortable using your meeting platform and other tools, see Chapter 21).

Let's now have a look at Duhigg's recommendations to managers leading a meeting.

Avoid interrupting team members

How many times have you interrupted someone because of a delay in the connection? Not interrupting others can be harder in online meetings than in colocated ones.

A first step towards reducing interruptions is to ask everyone to speak at the beginning of the meeting, so you can assess the quality of their broadband, and how well the meeting platform is operating. (There are other benefits, covered in Chapter 7.) You can also ask each other questions to see whether there are any gaps in the conversation caused by the tech, and adapt your rhythm to accommodate those delays in the connection.[26]

In addition, remember that silence feels longer in the online space. Someone pausing for breath or trying to articulate a thought might come across as having finished speaking. If in doubt, you can always say something along the lines of: "Can I double-check that you've finished what you were saying?"

---

26   Sometimes when I watch the news, I have great fun assessing the quality of phone lines and
       other communication infrastructures during the items involving foreign correspondents, by
       paying attention to the unnatural pauses caused by a few seconds' delay.

If you want to add something to what someone is saying, before they move on to their next thought, you can type in the chat box, for example: "Let me know when you're done, I have something to add." This allows the speaker to bring you into the conversation at the appropriate time, freeing you up to concentrate on what they are saying, instead of focusing on finding the right time to speak.

Admit what you don't know

Here is where we are at an advantage in the online space. We can admit that we don't know something; but if we know where to click on our browser or computer to top up our knowledge, we can find the answer almost straightaway.

If someone asks something that you can quickly check while you are online, just and check it. Be sure to communicate what you are doing ("I don't know the answer to that, but if you give me 10 seconds…"), and go look it up. If it's going to take you more than 30 seconds to find the answer you might as well make a note, look it up straight after the meeting, and add your findings to the online space where you follow up after meetings.

Don't end a meeting until everyone has spoken at least once

There are many reasons why people stay quiet in meetings, whether they are colocated or online. Sometimes, people feel as if everything which had to be said, has been – and they follow the ancient piece of advice: 'Don't speak unless you can improve the silence.' Or maybe they haven't formulated their thoughts completely, and don't feel ready to share them.

Sometimes, before moving the conversation along, you might need to hold the silence to give room for people to speak up. As mentioned previously, silence feels more uncomfortable in the online space, as people tend to stare at the screen when on video, and it is difficult to decipher what silence signifies during audio calls.

Be brave: hold that silence after you have asked if anyone has anything further to add. Count to five if you must, even to ten. It might be the moment that the person who hasn't spoken yet decides to share their thoughts. (I cover more on this in Chapter 26.)

In Chapter 7, I suggest several ways in which to kick off the meeting with a question for everyone to take turns to answer. You can extend this 'round robin' into the meeting itself. In her book *Time to Think*, Nancy Kline suggests that when covering the first item in the agenda, everyone gets the chance to speak.[27] Make sure that the item is clear, and that the discussion doesn't start until everyone has had their chance to have their say.

Another way of ensuring that everyone speaks at the meeting is to do a round robin in the team before ending, asking everyone for a final word. Ask each person to nominate who should go next. You can do the same if you are on audio, or go down the list in the chat. If you have a list of names of those present, make sure you have ticked off everyone's name that list before you close the meeting. Finally, have a space where you can add your thoughts after the meeting has ended.

Encourage people to express their frustration without being judged

Sometimes we can't help it. When people express their frustration at something that is not working in the team, as managers we can feel personally attacked. But if we show our discomfort at team members sharing their discontent, they will be less likely to speak their minds again.

When online meetings are held on video, one disadvantage is that you can constantly see everyone and their reactions. In the colocated space, you can only take in a few faces at a time, but in the online world (at least for now, while we are still using 2D video), we are looking straight at everyone, *all* the time – which increases our need for self-awareness.

If you hear someone expressing discontent, double-check that you are not frowning or reacting in a way that might signal that it's not all right to continue speaking. Or if you catch yourself disapproving, focus on them instead. Take a deep breath, direct your attention to what they are saying (rather than on the effect that their words are having on you), and ask as many questions as you can to understand their context.

(It's also worth remembering that those in the meeting can't see the lower half of our bodies. If discomfort or impatience creeps in when someone else is speaking, how about letting it flow to your legs instead of your face?)

---

27   Nancy Kline (2002) *Time to Think*, Cassell Illustrated (Kindle Edition).

Call out intergroup conflicts, and resolve through open discussion

One could argue that it's not the manager's responsibility to resolve all conflicts in the team; it should be the team's responsibility to resolve their own conflicts. In addition, you could suggest that if managers point out and resolve conflicts all the time, team members will always wait for the manager to act when there is conflict between people, rather than resolve it themselves. However, as a manager, calling out conflict shows that we can work through our different opinions, and use them to improve our decision-making.

This is an aspect where this book can't guide you without understanding your team's dynamics and culture. You will have to be the judge of when it is necessary for you to 'call out intergroup conflicts and resolve through open discussion'.[28] What looks like conflict to you might look like healthy discussion to someone else. However, if people are disagreeing, and you are wondering whether to intervene, ask yourself:

- Is this discussion helpful to the work?
- Will it help us get better results, or to improve our team process?
- Is this a discussion that we need to hold right now, or should those involved schedule a time to seek agreement, or at least an understanding?

Disagreements are helpful when they lead to actions or decisions, otherwise they are just social activities.

Speaking of social activities, non-work-related conversations are good places to practise disagreeing with each other. For example, voicing your dislike of a sports activity that another team member loves can be done in a playful way. It can signal that 'just because I disagree with you doesn't mean I don't like you' – and this is a safe way of rehearsing disagreement for high-stakes situations. That is why it's important to put time aside for social conversations, either as separate meetings (such as 'virtual coffees', which I cover in Chapter 16) or at the beginning of regular meetings.

---

28   Duhigg, location 731.

Disagreeing with our team members about the work is an essential part of improving our process. Help people to stay focused on the task, and on how their disagreements can improve their collaboration and work. (You can find more guidance on this in Chapter 27 *When We Disagree*.)

MAKE YOUR MEETINGS MATTER

- At your next meeting, observe everyone's behaviour, including your own. How much does it align with the behaviours identified with psychological safety?
- What will help you to create an environment where team members feel psychologically safe? What kind of preparation will you need to do for your meetings? What set-up will you need?

<u>9</u>

Leading by example

In his book *Team of Teams*, General Stanley McChrystal describes how he role-modelled inclusive behaviour and the daily meetings his 'team of teams' held:

> Our daily Operations and Intelligence (O&I) video teleconference became key to my overall communications effort. Although the information exchanged was the baseline 'product,' the O&I served as my most effective leadership tool as well, because it offered me a stage on which to demonstrate the culture I sought.[29]

McChrystal goes on to tell the fascinating story of how he turned around one section of the US military by pulling people together around him, instead of taking on the role of decision-maker and leader-hero. He used these daily online meetings not just to make sure all the troops stayed aligned, but also to promote a flat organisation and culture of accountability and appreciation.

When young members of the command were responsible for the daily briefing, McChrystal would find out their names in advance, and put them at ease by addressing them by their first name. Throughout the meeting, he would carefully monitor his own behaviour to make sure he gave no indication of boredom, impatience or lack of attention. At the end of the briefing, he would ask the junior person a question to show that he had been listening attentively, and that their work mattered to him.

Role-modelling can be exhausting, but it gets easier with time. This is why you shouldn't abandon 'status meetings' or catch-up meetings in the online world. Although work progress can be reported via asynchronous

---

29   Stanley McChrystal, David Silverman, Tantum Collins and Chris Fussell (2015) *Team of Teams: New Rules of Engagement for a Complex World*, Penguin (Kindle Edition), location 227.

communication, progress meetings tend to be less energy-consuming than other meetings. They allow you to concentrate on role-modelling those behaviours that contribute to team success. They are also spaces where you can rehearse those behaviours that don't come naturally to you.

As McChrystal says:

> The rules for any meeting are established more by precedent and demonstrated behavior than by written guidance. I wanted the O&I to be a balance of reporting of key information and active interaction. That didn't come naturally, particularly across a digital medium. The participants came from different organizational cultures, were thousands of miles apart, and had never met in-person. Getting candor under those conditions was not easy, but we made it work.[30]

It seems like McChrystal was behaving in a way that generated psychological safety in his meetings online.

WHEN NOT TO LEAD BY EXAMPLE

When we regularly champion our team's success, when we understand how our work fits into the organisation's aims, and when we feel comfortable in our team, it's only human to want to be the person that comes up with bright ideas, the one who saves the day. But in some cases, this can be damaging to teamwork.

Liz Wiseman, author of *Multipliers: How the Best Leaders Make Everyone Smarter*,[31] suggests that: 'Someone idea rich can lead to others being idea lazy.'[32] With the best of intentions, leaders get in the way of people's intelligence by continuously generating ideas, rather than by

---

30   McChrystal, location 4041.

31   Liz Wiseman (2017) *Multipliers: How the Best Leaders Make Everyone Smarter*, HarperCollins.

32   Leading Saints (2017) 'What to do when the bishop is an accidental diminisher: An interview with Liz Wiseman', podcast, 12 May. Available at: https://leadingsaints.org/what-to-do-when-the-bishop-is-an-accidental-diminisher-an-interview-with-liz-wiseman/

asking questions and creating the space for others to feel as if they are required to use their full intelligence in the team.[33]

If you are a creative person who thinks easily on their feet, resist the temptation to save the day in your team by being the first to generate new ideas and come up with solutions. Make room for others to have the time to think, for lightbulbs to ignite. Be comfortable with silence, and avoid always being the first person to break it. If you are constantly the one coming up with innovative ideas and next steps, your team members will get used to that. They won't see the point in bringing their full intelligence to the meeting – and your meetings will stop mattering to them.

FLATTENING THE HIERARCHY

> A meeting is a status arena. It is no good to pretend that people are not or should not be concerned with their status relative to the other members in a group. It is just another part of human nature that we have to live with.[34]

This quote comes from a *Harvard Business Review* article published in 1976, before email and collaboration platforms. And yet doesn't it still ring true?

Consciously or not, when we come together as a group, there might be a tendency to establish a pecking order, or to revert to role. For example, if we are seen as 'the funny one' in the group and we like that, we might try to reaffirm that view by joking. Or if we are seen as the group's 'coordinator', others might reaffirm that role by always waiting for us to pull the group together to decide who will do what. The dynamics that have always been inherent in colocated teams are also visible in the online space.

Here is an example that Simon, a project management consultant, shared with me:

> You know, I often would be the only one in the meeting with my camera on – but as soon as a senior manager joined the meeting

---

33   David Burkus (2017) 'Liz Wiseman: How the best leaders make everyone smarter', *Radio Free Leader*, podcast. Available at: http://davidburkus.com/2017/07/0820-how-the-best-leaders-make-everyone-smarter-with-liz-wiseman/

34   Antony Jay (1976) 'How to run a meeting'. *Harvard Business Review* 54(2): 43–57, p. 45.

and turned on their video, others would follow. I also noticed that the higher up in the organisational chart people were, the more likely they would be to turn their video on.

PROMOTING COLLABORATION

We can't control what others do or how they fulfil their own social needs during meetings. What we can do as managers or team leaders is to use meetings to role-model the collaboration behaviours that we would like to see in our team. Like it or not, team members' behaviour and group norms are heavily influenced by the manager's behaviour, either by adopting acceptable behaviours or rebelling against them.

The online space gives us the opportunity to work more autonomously (by providing all the information needed online), and to create teams where members feel accountable to each other, instead of only to their boss (through making progress and results visible).

Take a moment to reflect on whether you are reinforcing your organisational status in meetings. Are you always the one who:

- Opens and closes the meeting?
- Drives the agenda forward?
- Reigns everyone back in when the conversation goes off on a tangent?
- Decides who can speak next?

Think about it: from a team member's viewpoint, if the manager or team leader always looks after the team process, they don't need to monitor their behaviour as much (someone else will do that for them), they don't have to hold others in their team accountable when their behaviour is unproductive, someone else will step up – you get the picture.

It's worth distributing the responsibility for running a meeting among team members. You can start by allocating different roles.

MAKE YOUR MEETINGS MATTER

- What behaviours do you want to role-model in your team? Write them down and read them before your next meeting.
- Following the meeting, think: what behaviours did you role-model? Were any of them on the list?

<u>10</u>

Sharing roles

The first step to distribute responsibility for making your meetings successful is to make sure that you are not the only one with host or admin powers. Configure your meeting platform as much as possible, so that everyone can control how they take part.

For example, some platforms restrict attendees' use of the whiteboard, allowing only the host (or presenter) to use it. This restricts how attendees interact and engage in the meeting, so make sure these features are accessible to everyone, not just yourself. Avoid behaviours which can be seen as autocratic.

. . . .

I must confess that as meeting host, I find the power to mute others difficult to resist. On occasions, in the name of efficiency and productivity, I have muted someone else when their background noise was interfering with the meeting – a choice that, though drastic, was preferable to interrupting the conversation or sending a message in the chat.

When I have chosen to do this, I have made a point of telling the person and the group that I had muted them by exercising my host powers, and apologised for my hierarchical approach.

. . . .

ROTATE THE FACILITATOR/MEETING LEAD ROLE

You don't always have to be the one who facilitates or runs the meeting. If you have different meetings (updates versus strategy versus problem-solving), why not suggest that different people run a different type of meeting?

Some team members might be good at sticking to the agenda, others might have a knack for helping people build on each other's ideas, while others still might be talented at spotting when you need to change course in the middle of the meeting.

. . . .

INSPIRATION

At the distributed company Trello,[35] some teams rotate the facilitator role at every status update meeting. Their explanation:

'We rotate who leads the meeting because let's be honest, no one wants to hear the same person talk on and on all the time. This also gives everyone on the team a sense of ownership for the meeting.'[36]

. . . .

Besides enabling the manager to focus on the content of the meeting (rather than on the dynamics of the conversation), rotating facilitators can help team members to feel more ownership of the meeting, and appreciate the effort it takes to keep a meeting on track. Moreover, being in charge of a specific element of the group process can nurture leadership skills.

Leadership skills are useful for all team members to have. There might be times when the team needs to break down into informal, self-organised task forces, or when team members become part of cross-functional projects. Knowing that as a professional you are able to rally the troops can boost somebody's confidence, taking them onto a new level of performance.

As leadership is context-specific,[37] a meeting may be one context in which people can discover their ability to facilitate a discussion, or organise a group to take action. This confidence can ripple through to other areas of their work.

---

35   Trello is now part of the larger company Atlassian.

36   Stella Garber (2016) 'How to give your team meetings a status update', Trello, 14 April. Available at: https://blog.trello.com/give-team-meetings-status-update

37   In 'Growing Leaders', leadership specialist John Adair quotes a study from 1948 which concluded that 'leadership is a relationship that exists between persons in a social situation, and that persons who are leaders in one situation may not necessarily be leaders in other situations'. Ralph Stogdil, in John Adair (2009) *How to Grow Leaders: The Seven Key Principles of Effective Leadership Development*, Kogan Page (Kindle Edition), locations 619–621.

How often have you heard the question: 'Are leaders born or made?' Personally, I have always found that question to be irrelevant. When considering somebody's leadership potential, the first question to ask should be: 'Do they *want* to lead?'

Sometimes, the reason that people don't put themselves forward for spearheading an initiative or leading a project is that they have never had the chance to lead, and so doubt their ability to do so. In a supportive team, running a meeting is a contained, safe arena where it is easy to practise and receive feedback. Meetings, especially regular ones, can be a safe place for team members to develop their leadership skills.

Developing team members' leadership skills can have benefits beyond our internal team operations. Anyone in your team could end up having a conversation with someone else in the organisation, a client or vendor, where they can advocate for your team – or at least show it in good light. This is part of leadership: understanding the strengths and limitations of your team to represent it in the best possible way.

In an environment where we don't see each other every day, we want team members to proactively gather information about what others are doing, and stay connected to the rest of the team: team members can't rely on the manager to do this all the time, especially in a distributed environment. Leading team meetings can be a safe way to boost people's confidence, and help them take ownership of the team.

PLAYING DIFFERENT ROLES

In a *21st Century Work Life* podcast episode,[38] virtual team facilitator Nancy Settle-Murphy shares how she had helped a leader of a virtual team to delegate the responsibility of running meetings to the rest of the team. Nancy broke down the different responsibilities of the team leader, and suggested that team members took on specific roles during the meetings. For example, one person ended up in charge of timekeeping, while another was tasked with bringing the conversation back on track when it derailed.

---

38   Virtual Not Distant (2017) 'WLP107: Facilitating virtual meetings', podcast, 26 January. Available at: www.virtualnotdistant.com/podcasts/facilitating-virtual-meetings

This can be a good place to start in a team not used to meeting online, or where meetings have always been run by the manager. Team members become aware of the different aspects that make meetings successful, and the responsibility to run them starts to be distributed.

Once you can share the responsibility of preparing the agenda, driving the discussion forward, giving people their turn to speak and making sure the meeting ends on time, you can concentrate on role-modelling behaviours that will help create psychological safety and promote collaboration.

ROLES THAT TEAM MEMBERS CAN TAKE

As your team meets regularly, you'll refer to your team charter less often. In a similar way, as you become more comfortable with meeting online, different team members can swap roles from one meeting to another.

In 'traditional' (as in manager-led and colocated) team meeting set-ups, the manager takes almost every role available: chair, timekeeper, gatekeeper, participant, facilitator, etc. They might even be taking notes and sharing them later with the team.

If your meeting involves more than seven people, it might be a good idea for different people to take on different types of responsibility and to make the meeting efficient. However, in smaller teams, dividing these roles in the way suggested below might feel artificial – but you never know, it might work for you.

Even if you are an experienced team, if you need to have longer, more complex discussions, consider allocating roles to different people to help you stay on track. You can swap around at each meeting, or you can take the same role at every meeting. Here are a few to consider.

Leader/Owner

Some meetings will be of more importance to some people than others; issues will be raised that will affect some more than others. If you are covering a specific issue in the meeting and one of your team members is going to be directly affected by it, or is very familiar with it, it might be a good idea for them to lead the meeting. In that way, they can make sure that essential points are covered, and key decisions are made.

Alternatively, it might be more appropriate for someone less involved with the issue to facilitate the meeting, as they can maintain an objective viewpoint and keep the conversation balanced.

Timekeeper

What this role entails is obvious, but it's important to give the timekeeper licence to interrupt. This means that they won't get stern looks when they halt someone halfway through an important point. You can agree within your team how they should intervene: in the chat box, verbally, through hand gestures, by playing music – be as creative as you want to be.

Note-taker

If you need to keep a record of what happened at your meeting, the note-taker can take down any decisions made or key information conveyed, and share them later with the rest of the team. Make sure they can still contribute to the meeting, and that they are muted as they type away!

Videokeeper

If you are recording the meeting, it's worth having one person who is responsible for this, and for sharing the video or audio later. Make sure this person has all the admin powers necessary to do this.

Valet

This is the person in charge of the 'parking lot': the area where all the great ideas that can't be actioned or discussed immediately are parked. They look out for those ideas throughout the discussion that might belong to this space. For example:

"You know, it seems to me like we've mentioned three times now that in order to pursue that idea, we'd first need to finish our current project. Should we park it?"

It can be their responsibility also to make sure that those ideas are not forgotten about.

Health-checker

One thing that differentiates colocated meetings from team meetings is that even shorter meetings can have an effect on our health. Staring at the screen for a fixed period, not moving our heads from the same position for a while, can become uncomfortable. As in most of our life, we sometimes forget about the importance of looking after our health.

The Health-checker's responsibility is to remind the team when a break is due, possibly even to lead a little stretch or exercise to loosen up the neck and shoulders.

As with all new practices, you can try this role allocation a few times, evaluate whether it's useful, and decide whether or not to continue using it.

YOUR OWN TEAM

What are your thoughts as you look at this list of roles? Is it overcomplicating the meeting process? Maybe, but even if you end up leading the meeting yourself, this list should give you an idea of your different responsibilities – make sure you don't let any slip.

Carrying out these roles successfully involves careful listening and observation of what's going on in the meeting. It requires team members to connect with the team's energy and dynamics. If your team hasn't planned or designed anything together for a while, taking on these roles might help to tune into group dynamics once again.

Warning!

It could be argued that there is a danger of becoming so involved in fulfilling these roles that we don't pay any attention to the content of the meeting! Just be sure to check in with each other regularly, to make sure this isn't the case.

MAKE YOUR MEETINGS MATTER

- What roles do you take in meetings? If you are taking all of them, how about asking the team to take up some of them?
- Consider doing this for the next complex meeting.
  Evaluate at the end of the meeting how it went, and plan for the next one.

11

Enrich communication with video, communicate frequently with audio

A new team might benefit from video meetings as team members get to know each other, work out the team's norms of communication, and learn to 'listen between the lines'. (Remember that every time a person joins your team, you effectively become a new team.)

A mature (in both attitude and tenure), high-trust team can hold audio meetings regularly without affecting team relationships. Team members will feel comfortable already with inadvertently interrupting each other: they will have learned how to pass the baton in a conversation and intuit what others are feeling, just from the tone of their voice.

In any case, a video meeting where everyone can see each other gathered together online can reignite team spirit. Being able to see everyone together on a screen is important if the nature of the work means that team members regularly work on separate tasks, or if the work is fragmented. When there is no need to communicate about the work, the cadence of communication can decrease, leaving some team members feeling isolated or disconnected from the rest.

On top of that, if the whole team never gathers together online, it can start to feel unhealthy. Even if employees don't need to collaborate with others day-to-day, they might still need a strong visual reminder that they share a common purpose with others.

MEETING WITHOUT WEBCAMS

Meeting over video becomes difficult when internet connections are dodgy, or office spaces are not set up to accommodate webcam use. In these cases, it might be preferable to switch to an audio-only meeting, even if only one team member is having problems with their video.

When you switch to an audio-only environment, think about the information that will be lost, and find ways to replace it with verbal cues or language. There are certain things we do when talking to others of which often we are not aware: we smile, nod, frown. When we can't see each other's faces, this kind of communication is lost.

When relying only on audio for your meetings, try articulating some of these non-verbal cues. For example:

- If you find yourself smiling, give a little laugh, giggle or just say, "I'm smiling".
- Saying "I'm smiling" invites your team members to visualise your face, as one way of bringing visual language into people's minds.
- Use "Hmm" or "Yes", instead of nodding to yourself. Or say, "I'm nodding."
- Use your hands as you speak, to animate the voice.
- Agree in the team on a phrase that communicates when you have finished speaking, so that others know they can take their turn.
- If you hear anything unusual in a person's background noise, such as birds tweeting, ask about it. As mentioned previously, this helps to get a picture of where the person is located. Visualising where a person is, or their environment, can reduce a feeling of distance.

If you are having a difficult conversation, check in with each other: "Can I just ask how we're getting on? As we can't see each other's faces, shall we just pause for a moment and check how we're feeling about this?"

One way of capturing facial expressions lost over audio is to pause the conversation and ask the team: "What's your facial expression right now?" In a high-trust environment, you might hear things like, "I'm frowning", "I just rolled my eyes", "I'm nodding". Sometimes communicating what we are doing is easier than saying how we are feeling – and it's easier to do both when we pause the meeting to check in with each other.

USE THE MEDIUM THAT SUITS YOUR TEAM BEST

When you attend a video meeting, as soon as more than one person appears on your screen, usually you see their faces smaller than when you sit next to them. This can feel like they are distant because in the 3D space, small things tend to be far away. In contrast, if you hold an audio call and you are wearing a headset (and the audio is decent), the person will seem to be closer to you than if you were sitting next to them. Something to consider.

Don't hop onto video just because you have heard it's the thing to do when working remotely, and don't stick to audio just because that is how it was always done in your organisation before high-bandwidth internet connections and affordable meeting platforms were widely available.

Use both video and audio-only mediums in ways that are in line with what you want to achieve and with the levels of trust that exist, or that you want to nurture in your team. Decide what is best for you – and even if you do decide that you should all turn on your webcams by default, respect those people who prefer to stick to audio-only every now and then.

. . . .

In the episode 'Meetings are Toxic' of the ReWork podcast, a guest shared her experience at a previous company. She was part of a team of homeworkers in a small business, where the CEO insisted they all met every day over audio for a 15-minute 'stand-up' meeting.

In principle, this sounds like a good idea, perfect for keeping everyone aligned. The problem was that meetings were always scheduled for a time convenient for the CEO, even though employees were spread all over the world, and some of them had children.

Due to the diverse time zones, some parents ended up having the meeting at 6am, just as their children were getting ready to go to school. On top of this, the content of the meetings was close to useless: people mainly reading updates which had already been shared online, and they frequently filled a whole hour.

You can imagine the silences generated in these meetings as the energy plummeted – and any motivation to contribute to the discussion (what discussion?) slowly faded away. What do you think the CEO did to tackle this downward spiral?

Demand that everyone switch their video on. Even though some team members were attending at 6am. With kids running around the house. With their faces barely lit, as daylight hadn't yet entered the house.

Talk about building trust and happiness at work.[39]

. . . .

MAKE YOUR MEETINGS MATTER

- How do you feel about using video? Do you know how others in your team feel about it?
- If you rarely use video in your meetings, give it a try – but make sure you give everyone plenty of warning.

---

39   Adapted from ReWork (2018) 'Meetings are toxic', podcast, 20 February. Available at: https://rework.fm/meetings-are-toxic/

12

Before you press record...

Most meeting platforms have a recording feature, but even if the software does not have one built-in, there are simple ways in which you and team members can capture audio (and even video) by using screen-capturing software. However, just because it's easy to record a meeting, and it's the easiest way of capturing everything that happens in it, does not mean that you should press that record button lightly.

Recording is a good idea when those who can't make the meeting want to follow the full conversation instead of reading the meeting notes. This can be useful not just from an accuracy viewpoint (where meeting notes have to be interpreted, for example), but also with team cohesion, as the person away from the meeting can 'reconnect' with everyone else as they watch the recording.

While recordings should not be a way to get out of attending meetings, they can enable team members who are travelling, or who need to change their schedule due to personal circumstances, to feel as if they are still taking part. Moreover, watching meetings held by sub-teams or task teams can give others insight into what their colleagues are working on: it is one way of making teamwork visible, and a good alternative to attending a meeting where team members know they have nothing to contribute.

One of our responsibilities as a team member is learning both about how our colleagues work and how everyone's work fits together. While we don't need to attend every meeting held in our team or be part of every single interaction, sometimes it is useful to watch or listen to a conversation. Catching up on conversations is the type of work that can be done during the least productive moments of the day.

ONCE YOU PRESS RECORD

If you are going to record a meeting for someone to watch later, acknowledge that this is happening. Keep in mind your absent colleague during the meeting, and find ways of involving them in the conversation.

- Are there any questions the viewer could answer?
- Do they need to contribute to the discussion in any way?

Vocalise this during the meeting (for example, "Louise, we know you've been having conversations with other teams in the organisation, have you got any thoughts on this?"), and make clear the action you would like the team member to take. Give them a time by which you would like them to communicate with the team, and signpost them to an area in your ecosystem to continue the conversation.

. . . .

BUILDING THE TEAM

I worked at a company where we recorded interviews with candidates applying for jobs. While watching one of those meetings, I realised that recording interviews was a great way of involving everyone in the organisation (12 of us) in the recruitment process without intimidating the interviewee.

Watching the interviews, it was easy to get to know the candidate and assess whether they might be a good match with the role and company. In this way, everyone who wanted to be involved in candidate selection could be part of the discussion.

What was even more interesting was watching fellow team members' behaviour during the interview. It was useful to hear how they introduced themselves and their roles, and how they described what it was like to work at the company. Sometimes they adopted a different persona when interacting with the candidate, and this was revealing.

When you interview someone, you try to show yourself and the company in the best light. I got to hear why people were proud of the company, and what they enjoyed the most about working there.

(If you decide to record interviews as part of your recruitment process, don't forget to let candidates know, and reassure them that the recordings will be only used internally.)

. . . .

Recordings of past meetings can be used to onboard new team members, or those joining halfway through a project. While newcomers can catch up with task progress through collaboration platforms and text documents, listening to recent conversations enables them to understand their team members better. In addition, it can give them an insight into team dynamics and how meetings are being run.

Yes, but…

By now you are probably thinking: *'This all sounds great, but I'm not sure we should record our meetings. Won't it inhibit what people say, and how they behave?'*

Yes, it will. In the same way as we pay attention to how we write emails because they stay on permanent record, knowing that a meeting is being recorded can affect how we behave. If you record meetings regularly, you are likely to forget that the camera is on, and behave as normal. But when deciding to record a meeting, you and your team need to be mindful that it could affect your feeling of safety and willingness to take risks – so again, don't press that 'record' button lightly. Knowing that a meeting is being recorded can prevent people from expressing their personal opinions, freely disagreeing with each other, and even exploring their creativity. In short, it can inhibit psychological safety.

Another thing to look out for is whether team members start to drop out of meetings, knowing they can watch the recording later. This could be a sign that team members feel as if their presence won't make a difference to the discussion. In this case, you need to examine carefully the conversations happening in your meetings, and look for ways of balancing team member contributions.

Whether you record some of your meetings will be entirely up to you and your team. You might have time zone issues,[40] or a few of you might need to make a decision affecting the whole team that you want others to know about. In these cases, treat recordings with respect, and consider deleting them after a week or so. Protect your meeting space, your conversations and continue valuing real-time interaction.

MAKE YOUR MEETINGS MATTER

- What is the make-up of your team? Is there little schedule overlap? Might you benefit from recording your meetings? If so, which ones?
- Always consider the trade-off between the benefits of making a recording available to those team members not present, and the need for privacy and psychological safety.

---

40   If your team members are spread over different time zones that makes having meetings difficult, consider switching to asynchronous communication. For how one team in Buffer did this, check out Victoria Gonda (2020) 'What happened when our team switched to only asynchronous meetings', Inside Buffer. Available at: https://open.buffer.com/asynchronous-meetings/

13

Unmuted by default

I am not sure when it became common practice, but I often find that people mute themselves by default at the beginning of online meetings, even if they are attending from a quiet place. It's probably a practice carried over from having conference calls in the office from a noisy desk. Or it might be a reaction to meeting platforms where attendees are 'spotlit'[41] as soon as their microphone detects a noise, such as a cough or pen tapping on the desk.

There are times, such as when you are in a noisy environment, when it's preferable to mute your microphone; but if you are in a quiet space with no background noise, why would you mute yourself?

. . . .

When I mentioned this in a workshop, one participant immediately crossed his arms and frowned.

"You don't agree?" I asked.

He shook his head and said, "Heavy breathers."

He explained that often, one person in his team would breathe heavily into his headset microphone, which in effect meant breathing heavily into other people's ears. I challenged the participant.

"Why don't you just ask him if he can move the microphone a little further away from his mouth?"

He shook his head again.

I sympathise. It's difficult to bring up the fact that someone's breathing is bothering you. We don't want to cause friction or make others uncomfortable. But the answer is not to establish unnecessary norms to avoid a small amount of discomfort. If

---

41   In some meeting applications such as Google Hangouts, the person speaking takes up most of the screen, pulling everyone's focus.

our microphones are muted by default we can avoid the heavy breathing, but we might also damage team communication.

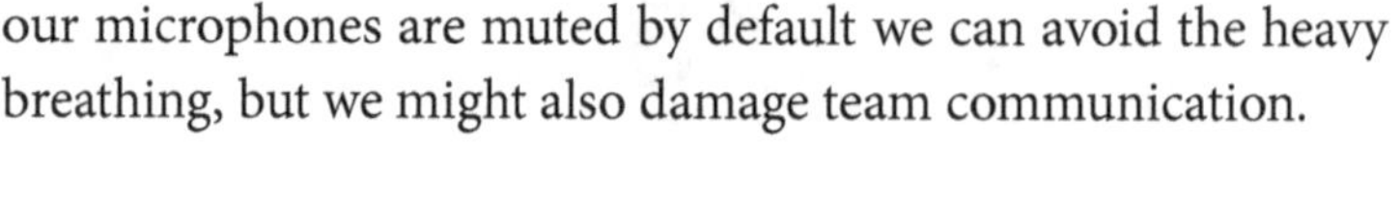

COMMUNICATION PATTERNS IN HIGH-PERFORMANCE TEAMS

In 2012, Alex Sandy Pentland, Director of MIT's Human Dynamics Laboratory, shared the findings from a study analysing the communication patterns of colocated, high-performing teams in organisations. Pentland and his team spent seven years recording the movement, tone of voice and interactions of more than 2,500 employees in 21 organisations. [42]

Those taking part in the study wore a sociometric badge which measured when people were talking, their tone of voice, their position relative to others and their body language. Surprisingly, the data collected during team meetings showed that one characteristic of high-performance teams was that side conversations took place, with vocalised responses (such as 'Aha', 'Mmm', 'Totally') when someone else was speaking.

It is this last aspect of team communication which makes me think team that members muting themselves throughout a meeting can damage communication. Muting microphones removes those spontaneous sounds of agreement and expressions of doubt that help communication flow, and increase a sense of connection.

The communication cycle

The information that flows between us during communication helps us to adapt the conversation as we go along. The verbal content ('hardcore' information such as facts, opinions, etc.) is only one component of communication. As we speak, we look out for signs that tell us whether people are following what we are saying, whether they disagree with us and the impact we might have on them.

Some signs we look out for are spontaneous reactions: laughter, vocalisations of surprise ("Er?" "What?"), strong disagreement ("Er... not me"), sounds of agreement, etc. If people mute themselves by default,

---

42   Alex Sandy Pentland (2012) 'The new science of building great teams'. *Harvard Business Review* 90(4): 60–70.

no background noise is present to interfere with the conversation, then we are removing an essential part of communication and breaking the feedback loop.

Open mic

In addition to keeping non-verbal audio communication channels open, open microphones can enable engagement (Figure 7).

Figure 7: Communication flow with open microphones

As mentioned in Chapter 7, one difficulty of having online conversations is that it's easy to inadvertently interrupt someone. However, sometimes these interruptions are beneficial. For example, a question might pop into our head which will clarify what we're hearing straightaway, or we might contribute a piece of information that changes the course of what the speaker is saying.

Having a microphone on mute can stop us from contributing to the conversation spontaneously. On the one hand, if we need to unmute ourselves every time we want to intervene, however small our contribution, by the time we reach for the mouse, hover over the unmute button and press the tiny thing, the moment has passed. On the other hand, if you are someone who has so many fleeting thoughts that you end up interrupting others more than you would like to, muting your microphone might help you be more mindful of your interruptions.

VIDEO IS NOT ENOUGH

Here is one final point in my quest to debunk the myth that muted microphones are best.

. . . .

Not long ago, I was running a session at an internal conference for Virtual Team Talk, an online community. There were about ten of us online, with our webcams turned on. I was sharing my screen, so I could only see four faces in tiny windows, and everyone else was hidden from view.

As I was talking and leading the conversation, I realised how quiet it was. Because everyone's mics were muted, I couldn't 'feel' anyone with me, I was getting no feedback. There was just silence. People were nodding and smiling, but I couldn't see them.

Being in a safe environment, I mentioned that the silence was really off-putting, as I felt like I was disconnecting from everyone in the meeting.

Over the next few minutes, I noticed a change. For a start, one of the community members started to listen actively by letting out sounds of agreement. (Active listening shows that you are paying attention to the person speaking. It is a skill traditionally associated with the colocated space, but can be easily adapted to the online environment.)

Deliberately contributing non-verbal sounds when someone is speaking can show that you are listening and tell the speaker how the message is being received. Even when we are on video, we can't rely on the speaker to get all our non-verbal information from our facial expressions. Adding sound to the mix can enrich our communication.

. . . .

I am not suggesting that everyone at meetings starts making sounds to show that they are listening to the speaker (although sometimes, this might be useful); rather, that we should allow our spontaneous reactions to come through. If we want our online meetings to matter as much as their colocated counterparts (or more!), we need to find ways of enriching our communication, not dampen it – so unless you are in a noisy space, go on, leave your microphone open.

MAKE YOUR MEETINGS MATTER

- What is the norm in your team regarding microphone muting?
- At your next meeting, be aware to what extent people interact non-verbally with each other. Is there more room for team members to show signs of agreement, for example? For spontaneous sounds of laughter, surprise, outrage, etc. to come through?

14

Are we speaking the same language?

The advantage of holding meetings online is that we can hook up with people anywhere in the world. If proficiency in your team's official language varies greatly among its members, meetings can become a place of unequal contribution. Even when we transcend geographical borders and build a strong team identity, differences in language proficiency can get in the way of fruitful conversation.

How to navigate geographical cultural differences is beyond the scope of this book,[43] but it can at least assist in reducing the impact that language diversity has on your meetings.

SUBTLE DIFFICULTIES

When a country is renowned for its comfort with speaking other languages, it is easy to assume that its nationals are comfortable expressing themselves in another language.

. . . .

A few years ago I worked for a Swedish company, where everyone spoke almost perfect English, so I paid no attention to the fact that it was not their native language. However, as the conversations I had with them became more complex, I realised that, especially when the conversation got difficult, language got in the way.

---

43   For excellent guidance on leading virtual teams, check out Nancy Settle-Murphy's website www.guidedinsights.com, or her book, *Leading Effective Virtual Teams* (Routledge, 2012). Also check out culture cubes in Theresa Sigillito Hollema (2019) 'Don't waste a cultural bridge!', Interact, 5 March. Available at: www.interact-global.net/category/working-across-cultures/culture-cubes/, and her book on leading global teams (she is working on it at the time of writing). Erin Meyer's *The Culture Map* is also worth a read, although it is aimed at in-person interactions.

Similarly, my mother-in-law, like most Dutch people, speaks excellent English. But in a recent heated discussion she said, "I'm having real difficulties expressing myself in English" – something I hadn't considered before.

. . . .

The advantage of having meetings as opposed to communicating asynchronously, is that you can get real-time feedback on whether you are being understood. If you are on video, you can watch how people react, or regularly check in during the audio-only conversation whether everyone is following. But this kind of communication can leave some people behind in the conversation, if we don't consciously adapt our behaviour.

To be inclusive in meetings, here are some behaviours you can adopt when there are different levels of language proficiency in your team.

Slow down

It's so easy to get carried away when we are in the middle of talking about something we feel strongly about, or when we are asking people to act with urgency. In these cases, we run the risk of important information getting lost, of ideas not being challenged, and of not giving space to people who might have something to add. In addition to this, technology glitches and unstable internet connections can increase difficulties in understanding. Moreover, if you are not used to listening to another language for long periods of time, you might feel disconnected.

Slowing down when speaking is an easy first step, to help those team members who find it hard to follow and contribute to the conversation. However, what might be harder is slowing down as a listener. This means giving people time to find the right words to express themselves, without becoming impatient. Slowing down our listening also involves checking that what we are hearing makes sense, and asking for clarification when we aren't sure whether we have understood correctly.

Mind your language

Slowing down also gives you the chance to check that you are not using words which can cause confusion. Avoid slang and acronyms that only some of your team members use regularly, and explain cultural references with which some people might not be familiar. If you are using unusual words or referring to people or places which some participants might not be familiar with, type them out in the chat box.

Plan for longer discussions

Nancy Settle-Murphy, who started facilitating meetings with global teams before Facebook was invented, adds 20–25% more time to the agenda when there are people on the call who are not proficient in the team's common language. This gives the group extra time for pausing, clarifying and paraphrasing.[44]

Create visual signals

Sometimes it's faster (and more fun) to ask someone to slow down or repeat the last thing they said by using a hand signal, instead of words. By agreeing at the beginning of a meeting on these hand signals, we are also acknowledging that there might be occasions when we need to hear something twice – it makes it acceptable to ask people to repeat or clarify what they said.

If you are working with a multicultural team, it might be worth including in your meeting charter how you will prevent those with less proficiency in your team's language from feeling excluded or disadvantaged in meetings.

Above all, remember that communication doesn't just consist of words. When we are meeting over video, we have a whole set of visual information to interpret; but even when the video is off, sounds of agreement and confusion helps us to understand what others think and feel.

. . . .

INSPIRATION

In *The Culture Map*, author Erin Meyer introduces the readers to Pedro Galvez, a Mexican manager leading a team with employees from a range of countries with very different communication norms.

44　I am grateful to Nancy Settle-Murphy for this information during review of the first draft of this book.

The team included people from both low-context cultures, where the message is delivered clearly and explicitly, and high-context ones, where the intent of a message is wrapped up in a set of shared assumptions.

To make sure that everyone had understood what had been said and/or agreed, Pedro would end the meetings with 'three levels of verification':

- One person would recap the key points orally. (This responsibility would rotate from one meeting to another.)
- Each person would summarise orally what they would do next.
- One person would send out a written recap, again on a rotating basis.

Although this example illustrates cultural differences in how we communicate, it is also a good example of how to make sure that everyone leaves the meeting knowing what has been agreed. Something to bear in mind, even if all your team members work in their native language.

. . . .

MAKE YOUR MEETINGS MATTER

- Be aware at your next meeting: are those more skilled in the language dominating the conversation?
- Are people struggling with the language being given enough time by everyone to express themselves?

15

Relationships wrap-up

Before we move on to the first of our meeting structures, the 'virtual coffee', let's recap the meeting principles which can strengthen relationships in your team.

Is there anything you can add or remove from your meetings to increase a sense of autonomy, competence or relatedness in your team members?

What kind of information not directly connected to your tasks can help team members feel more connected to each other, and help them to know each other better?

How regularly do team members ask questions and express their concerns, or offer new ideas in meetings? A lack of these might signal a lack of psychological safety. If this is the case in your team, make changes to how you run your meetings.

Be aware of how you behave in your meetings, and make sure you distribute responsibility for making them matter.

When do you use video-only or audio-only? How frequently do you mute yourself in a conversation? Would using your webcam or microphone differently enrich your communication in any way?

When choosing to record a meeting, consider how this might affect the conversation and the importance given to attending it.

If team members have different proficiencies in your organisation's official language, make sure you take account of this when planning and running your meetings.

To end this part of the book on relationships, three formats will guide you through different types of meetings:

- 'Virtual coffees' – meetings designed to strengthen the social bonds between team members.
- Pairing up – a system to orchestrate networking within your organisation.
- One-to-ones – you will probably run your online one-to-ones in a similar way to your colocated ones, but this chapter might inspire you to make some subtle changes.

16

Virtual coffees

Think of the many times you've had a little anecdote to share in a meeting, but you held back because it wasn't work-related and you didn't want to derail the conversation. Our anecdotes, stories and broad range of interests all communicate who we are: they make us three-dimensional people rather than two-dimensional colleagues. That is where virtual coffees come in.

Virtual coffees are online informal gatherings, just like sitting across from colleagues at a coffee table at work, or when you pop over to a local café for a short break. Having a virtual coffee feels different from sitting across a coffee table, but the aim is the same: to create space for a relaxed, informal chat.

An optional ('optional' here is key), regular slot for your team helps you all get to know each other better, and to get used to having different conversations online. If team members rarely need to talk to each other because their tasks are not interdependent, virtual coffees can facilitate team cohesion. By providing another avenue to connect with each other, these online meetings build fuller relationships between team members, making it easier to ask for help during day-to-day work.

If your team is relatively small (say, under five or six people), then you might not need to schedule these sessions. You might find the time to catch up with personal matters, or to share stories as they come up in your regular meetings. Maybe you arrange these social gatherings spontaneously, when the mood hits you.

However, for larger teams or virtual organisations, if these meetings aren't scheduled in advance, they might never happen. Planning when to have a coffee might feel artificial, but as with many remote conversations and practices, if you don't schedule them in, they will never happen. I refer to this concept as 'planned spontaneity'.[45]

If you like the idea of having regular virtual coffees, or you think it might help team members feel closer together and safer with each other, here are some suggestions on how to run them.

NAME THESE MEETINGS

'Virtual coffee' already has a nice ring to it, but you can make these sessions unique to your team by coming up with a different name for them. While not necessary, this is an opportunity to give your team a shared history and language. Some companies match the labels of these sessions to their culture: 'virtual beers', 'happy hour' or 'impromptu hours', the term used at Buffer for their slots for random conversation.

. . . .

INSPIRATION

At Happy Melly, for example, these non-work-related meetings were called 'Kitten Talk'. When the sessions were first set up, they were referred to as virtual coffees. But one day Lisette Sutherland, their remote office manager, turned up for the weekly ritual and found the meeting room empty.

Trying to "lure others online" (her words), she went over to the collaboration platform and started posting pictures of cute kittens. One other member was also online.

"Kittens? Did somebody say kittens? I love kittens!" she typed away, and off she went to the meeting room.

Lisette found another team member to have coffee with, and Kitten Talk was born.[46]

. . . .

---

45   'Planned spontaneity' is one of the concepts which make up 'visible teamwork'. The other two are 'deliberate communications' and 'work visibility'. It's a total concept which I will outline and explore further in my next book, *Leading through Visible Teamwork*.

46   Personal communication (conversation) on the online Virtual Team Talk community with Lisette Sutherland.

MAKE THEM OPTIONAL

I once freelanced for a company that regularly organised virtual coffees. The thought of turning up to an online meeting, not knowing who would be there or where the conversation might end up, was not something I always looked forward to – but I would force myself to attend those sessions regularly and, once I was there, actually enjoyed myself. I was glad I had made the effort.

(Although I have to say, on the few occasions when no one else turned up, I was secretly relieved – I had shown goodwill in attending, but didn't have to go through the small talk.)

There is an argument for making all meetings optional, and it applies doubly to these. If you feel like your time would be better spent doing something else, then you shouldn't be having coffee. However, when you remember that these sessions will be important for some team members, it's worth making the effort to turn up regularly.

Meeting others online and talking about the weekend, outdoor activities, hobbies, family and other random stuff can be a bond-forming experience that many people need, so as to feel connected to those they rarely (or even never) get to meet in the flesh (Figure 8).

Figure 8: Having a 'virtual coffee'

THE VALUE OF UNSTRUCTURED DISCUSSION

Besides providing team cohesion and an opportunity to connect with team members at different levels, virtual coffees also give online workers the space to build their communication skills.

During these informal chats, team members might learn new ways of 'passing the baton' between them. You might have a set of rules for your formal meetings, or your team might regularly rely on one person at the meeting to facilitate the conversation, but during virtual coffees you can discover unstructured ways of conversing.

At non-work-related meetings, as we hear things that rarely come up in meetings, we become more curious and listen more closely: the relaxed, informal tone helps the conversation flow, with no one facilitating it. As we navigate the conversation, what we learn subconsciously about each other's communication styles could make its way into our work-focused meetings, and remove the need to have someone always orchestrating the conversation.

Finally, people tend to suppress their emotions less during informal exchanges than in work settings. Think about it: when team members gather to spend time together and connect socially, they tend to laugh more and louder. They relive their anecdotes as they tell them. They show how much a recent event has upset them. Talking to each other without worrying about the outcomes of a conversation or getting through an agenda helps us to express ourselves more freely, and allows more of our personality to surface.

PROTECT YOUR COFFEE TIME

You might be tempted to hijack these meetings when you hit a busy period. "We really need to talk about that, but my diary is full. Why don't we put that on the agenda for our next virtual coffee?"

There is nothing wrong with agreeing to turn your coffee time into a work-focused meeting (it's your time together, you can do what you want with it!), but make sure that team members don't go along with your suggestion because it's easier to agree with you than to defend their virtual coffees. Furthermore, turning 'coffee time' into 'work discussion time' can signal that these moments are not important.

If you and your team value these kinds of social interaction, be sure to create the space for them. If scheduling this informal time together feels forced, find ways of facilitating spontaneous interaction, and commit to making them happen. For example, always keep your online status updated ('do not disturb', 'happy to have coffee', 'easy tasks') or decide on ways of signalling to others that you are doing light work and up for being invited online for coffee.

NOT JUST OVER COFFEE

Working on your relationships with your team members is something that you should do continuously, not just during these informal chats. Working together feels easier when we develop personal relationships with our team members; but mostly, team members look for managers who will help them through their work and support them.

Conversely, having a laugh with team members and being able to chat about non-work-related stuff is a bonus, but we shouldn't assume that this is a substitute for good, work-related conversations. It also isn't necessary to keep both kinds of conversations separate in your mind: it's possible to learn a lot about your team members from informal conversations, beyond what they choose to tell you. Pay attention to how they communicate: their language and frames of reference, and whether your interaction with them affects your own style of communication. Use this knowledge to help you improve your relationships, as you get on with your daily work.

Warning!

There is always a caveat. The main disadvantage of these coffee breaks is that while they might give us time out from our work, they don't give us a break from our screens. If your work involves spending all day at a computer, the last thing you want to do is take your break in front of it too. But if these interactions are important, find a way of making them work.

If you have been sitting at your desk all day, stand up and either switch to a wireless headset, or use your laptop's inbuilt speakers and microphone. Have a stretch and walk around; or if staying at your desk, change the position of your screen and adjust your posture. Stretch your fingers and arms during your virtual coffee time; if you need a complete break from your computer, leave the coffee session a bit earlier, take 10 minutes, then go back to your desk.

. . . .

INSPIRATION

At GitLab, the software development platform employing 200 people spread over 39 countries, employees are encouraged to have virtual coffee breaks for a few hours a week.

In addition to scheduled meetings, the company provides the space for spontaneous conversation and ad hoc coffee time. A virtual room ('random room') is permanently open for people to pop in and out, and accessible through a URL permanently posted in the random channel of their collaboration platform.[47]

. . . .

---

47   Sid Sijbrandij (2017) '"Virtual coffee" breaks encourage workers to interact like they would in an office', *Quartz at Work*, 6 December. Available at: https://work.qz.com/1147877/ remote-work-why-we-put-virtual-coffee-breaks-in-our-company-handbook/. GitLab (nd) 'GitLab Communication: Random'. Available at: https://about.gitlab.com/handbook/ communication/#random-room

17

Pairing up

In 2013, the research company Gallup found that close work friendships could raise employee satisfaction by 50%.[48] Although that statistic came from research carried out in the colocated space, potentially this could be the case in the remote space.

Good personal relationships contribute to better work conditions:

- Helping us feel safer
- Providing a different viewpoint, when we have problems with our work
- Fulfilling our social needs

In a way, having good working relationships should always be a part of our job descriptions.

Organising social time with everyone in a team, like virtual coffees, feeds team spirit. But there is also value in hopping online with just one other team member, to learn more about them as individuals. One-to-one interactions tend to be more relaxed than group ones, as it is easier to talk with one person online than with a group.

In remote teams and organisations, we need to find ways of helping these friendships develop. Just like bricks-and-mortar company dining areas are laid out to encourage people to mingle over lunch, it is useful to find ways for people across the organisation to connect. These interactions have both social and business functions: to help knowledge spread throughout the organisation.

There will be occasions when, no matter how much we value personal connection in a team, we will always find something else to prioritise.

---

48   Christine M. Riordan (2013) 'We all need friends at work', *Harvard Business Review*, 3 July. Available at: https://hbr.org/2013/07/we-all-need-friends-at-work

Systemising these meetings (like scheduling virtual coffees) can go a long way to preventing them from being cancelled when things get busy and stress creeps in – precisely the times when people need more support at work.

Having a system that takes care of the logistics (mainly, who needs to meet with whom, and by when) reduces the effort it takes to arrange and honour the meeting.

LET THE SYSTEM HELP BUILD RELATIONSHIPS

If you are transitioning from the colocated space, your team is new, or team members are afraid of infringing on others' time, there might be some benefit in setting up a system that takes the awkwardness out of arranging a virtual coffee between two team members. You can follow Trello's example.

· ·

INSPIRATION

With around 65% of Trello employees working remotely, it's difficult for many to cross paths with those with whom they don't directly work. To make sure that people had the chance to meet their co-workers, regardless of where they were physically based, the company came up with a pairing system called 'Mr Rogers'.1[49]

Through this system, employees are paired up on a Trello board open to the whole company. A 'card' (the unit in the board holding information) is created, two members are added to it, and a deadline is set by which the pair has to meet. The individuals can arrange a video meeting themselves to have an informal chat, or do something non-work-related. Following the meeting, employees write a couple of lines on their card about what they have been up to, so that everyone else in the company can find out more about them too.

---

49   Christine M. Riordan (2013) 'We all need friends at work', Harvard Business Review, 3 July. Available at: https://hbr.org/2013/07/we-all-need-friends-at-work

For Brian Cervino,[50] Product Marketing Manager at Trello, these calls helped him stop feeling like the company was made up of strangers. What's more, during one of these calls, he wrote a song with the person he had been paired up with, then shared it with everyone else. Brian is a musician, and this gave him the chance to make his talent visible in the organisation.

I like this system because it goes beyond expanding your internal network. By asking people to report back in public what they learned about each other, or what they got up to in their meeting, it helps others in the organisation learn more about them as people too.[51]

Setting up this system is simple, and team members can make the most of it by providing examples of how to shape the conversation. For example, individuals can introduce themselves, share something they have recently learned, whether a joyful moment or a new experience.

50   Virtual Not Distant (2016) 'WLP68: Brian Cervino talks about Trello and coffee!', podcast, 11 March. Available at: http://virtualnotdistant.com/trello-and-coffee/

51   I checked with Trello that even though it had been acquired by a larger company, people were still pairing up and getting benefit from these meetings. Atlassian's Twitter account replied: "We find it most useful for our remote teams and continue to enjoy the benefits the exercise provides teams all across Atlassian." https://twitter.com/AskAtlassian/status/1171083902842101760?s=20

OFFICIAL, BUT OPTIONAL

The fully distributed company, Buffer uses a similar, pairing-up system as part of its onboarding system. Newcomers are paired up with different people every week to prompt them to have meaningful conversations with a range of colleagues, including those they might not be working with directly.[52] This sends a strong signal: just because we are remote, doesn't mean that we don't encourage peer support and networking.

Similarly, Trello's 'Mr Rogers' was set up as an official programme: a dedicated person was responsible for setting up the pairs manually, showing that the company was prepared to allocate resources to facilitate informal interaction. The company has grown, and this responsibility has been passed on to a bot. You can easily delegate the process of matching up people to technology, as there are quite a few applications and tools available online which can randomly pair people up. They might take a bit of time to set up, but once they are configured, you are ready to go.

If you set up a similar system to the ones described here, you will need to commit to the programme, and review it regularly with your team. Make sure that everyone understands that attending these meetings is an important part of work, as it can build stronger relationships. Keep the programme optional, and make it easy for people to opt out for a period of time: for example, when they are busy or on holiday.

A SIDE BENEFIT: SKILL DEVELOPMENT

These informal one-to-one meetings can have several side benefits. For example, during larger team meetings, some people might never need to share their screen, place something in the chat or initiate a call. However, during these pairing sessions, they might need to do some of those things, prompting them to learn how to make better use of the platform.

Being able to use meeting platforms and applications will soon be a requirement of the 21st-century knowledge-worker. Using them during informal chat, where the focus is on connecting with the other person,

---

52   Arielle Tannenbaum (2020) 'A guide to conquering remote work loneliness from remote workers around the world', Buffer. Available at: https://open.buffer.com/remote-work-loneliness/

can remove some of the barriers that prevent people from connecting with others through technology.

Another side benefit of setting up these meetings in geographically distributed teams is getting to grips with scheduling meetings across different time zones. At Convert.com, team members[53] meet regularly for a 'buddy call': a 'designated, once-a-month chance to talk about anything but work. They are good practice for the Convert-honored art of navigating time zones and learning to make your calendar play well with others'.

---

53   At the time of writing, there are 12 full-time members working for Convert.com, with another 12 freelancers who might or might not want to join in the 'buddy system'. Source: Personal communication (via Chat) with Morgan Legge, 2017.

<u>18</u>

One-to-ones

Usually, a one-to-one conversation with a team member focuses on helping them achieve their objectives, but it is also an opportunity to strengthen your relationship with them. You can give them your undivided attention and listen to those concerns (and joys!) that they might not feel like sharing in another, more public, space.

One-to-ones don't always have to focus on performance. You can spend time talking about other professional areas, such as career development. Remote workers can be concerned about their progression in an organisation, because of a perceived lack of visibility. Through your own role as manager, you might know opportunities that exist within the company –such as being involved in cross-functional initiatives, or even job openings – of which your team members are not aware. Your one-to-ones are an occasion to find out more about the kind of information that remote team members lack, which will help them feel like they are in control of their career, or to do a better job though expanding their internal network.

When you are working with people remotely, it's tempting to postpone a one-to-one or move the focus away from feedback to something more time-sensitive. Unless there is a formal, regular process in place, discussions about an individual's development rarely happen. Without a regular feedback system, we are in danger of having a one-to-one only when something goes wrong. 'Feedback' can become synonymous with 'difficult conversation', and we miss out on the chance to give positive feedback to reinforce helpful behaviour and celebrate success.

Key to the success of this continuous feedback loop is holding one-to-ones regularly, even when there is not much to share. Having an allocated time to talk means that when things go wrong (and there is no urgency in fixing them), you already have a slot in place for a difficult conversation.

On top of this, remote workers are less likely to review their greatest successes with their managers than their colocated counterparts. Team members might be on their own at home when they finally solve a big problem; or they might be in an office surrounded by people who don't understand the importance of what they have completed. While team members don't want to blow their own trumpet, managers don't want to take up too much of their team members' time, and so keep their check-ins short.[54] Having a regular one-to-one gives team members the space to share pride in those achievements.

AGREE ON A STRUCTURE

To make sure that sharing achievement is part of regular one-to-one conversations, and that team members feel comfortable talking about them, is to set a slot for this during your conversations.

Make sure your one-to-ones are conversations, not one-way reports from either of you.

Find out:

- How the team member is doing
- What they are struggling with
- What they are proud of
- What they need from you

Mention any progress you have seen recently, and ask whether there are any blocks delaying progress. Point out any helpful team behaviours that have suddenly stopped, and find out the reasons for the change: some-times a change in behaviour is due to a change of context, which might be invisible to others in a remote team.

To help with the discussion, you can agree on a set structure for these conversations so that you always know how to kick them off. And on those days when you are thinking less clearly than normal or lacking energy, following a familiar set of steps will make it easier to converse. For example, you can adopt (and adapt) Automattic's '3-2-1-Oh' process.[55]

---

54   Annamarie Mann (2017) '3 ways you are failing your remote workers', Gallup, 1 August. Available at: www.gallup.com/opinion/gallup/214946/ways-failing-remote-workers.aspx

55   Jeremey Duvall (2016) 'Our current process for handling feedback', 5 October. Available at:

. . . .

INSPIRATION

At Automattic, most regular meetings between managers and team members follow the same structure. The team member reports on three things they have done well, two areas or skills which need improvement, and one way in which the team lead or manager and the organisation can support them. Finally, the 'Oh' prompts one or two sentences from the team member about what they are most excited or grateful for in the organisation, and how they would like to develop their career.

The '3-2-1-Oh' structure is perfect for short, regular conversations. They focus on helping the team member reflect on how they are doing, rather than waiting for the manager to comment on their progress. Team members can prepare in advance and share what is most important to them, rather than saying the first thing that comes to mind at the meeting, or taking the lead from their manager.

For those team members who are more reflective in nature, writing their thoughts might help them get the best out of the meeting.

. . . .

If you prefer longer conversations, you might want to adapt the structure they use at Buffer. This longer session requires more input from the team lead, but is still heavily weighted towards the team member's contribution.

. . . .

INSPIRATION

At Buffer meetings, for the first 10 minutes the team member shares and celebrates their achievements. This is followed by a 40-minute discussion, where they go into their current top challenges. The conversation then moves over to the team lead, who has 10 minutes to share their feedback, before shifting back to

---

https://jeremey.blog/sparta-feedback-process/

the team member, who has another 10 minutes to give feedback to the team lead.[56]

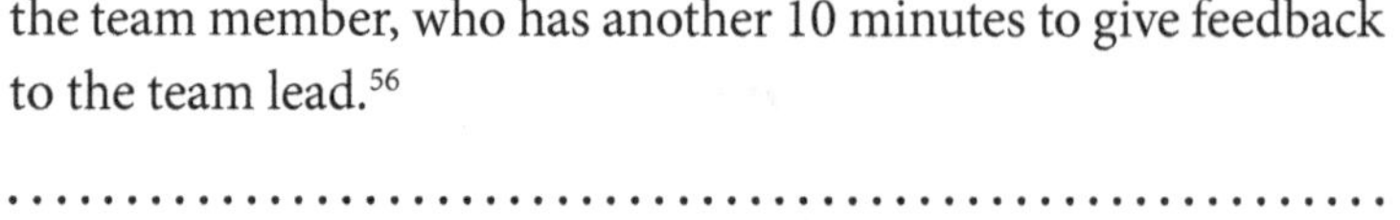

Having a structure removes some uncertainty of what these conversations can involve. It means we can spend less energy thinking about the 'agenda', and focus fully on the content.

ADAPT THE MEDIUM TO THE CONVERSATION

Hopefully you won't have many difficult conversations about team members' progress and development. However, there might be times when you have to address a performance or behaviour issue, when a team member is having problems with another team member, or even with how you are managing them.

Give some thought to the best medium to carry out a difficult conversation; don't just default to the communication channel you use in your team. While video offers both of you the opportunity to watch each other's reactions and to talk to each other without interruption, if either of your internet connections are unstable, technical glitches will affect your conversation.

Sometimes it's easier to find a suitable place from which to take a phone or audio call than to hold a video meeting. Also, take into account your own and your team member's preferences. Can you think better by focusing on the horizon? That would make an audio-only conversation preferable. Or does seeing the person you are talking to help you feel heard? Discuss with your team member how they prefer to have their one-to-ones, and adapt how you run them accordingly.

---

56   Joel Gascoine (2020) 'A simple guide to better coaching and feedback in your company', Buffer. Available at: https://blog.bufferapp.com/a-simple-guide-to-better-coaching-and-feedback-in-your-company

PART 3

THE MEETING

Introduction

Part 2 focused on making sure that our team meetings positively affect our relationships. This part will focus on running meetings that produce outcomes in the most effective way possible.

To start with, you need to know the outcome you are looking for. Is it:

- A decision?
- Buy-in for (or at least understanding of) a decision that has been made?
- Alignment at the beginning of a project?
- A project plan?
- A solution to a problem?

How you run your meeting depends on what both you and your team want to get from it. This will determine:

- Whether you put together an agenda or not (and if so, what kind)
- How long the meeting should be
- What structure it should take
- How much work you will all need to do beforehand (and afterwards)
- The tech you use during the meeting

As we look at starting and wrapping up a meeting, how to co-create an agenda and make decisions, don't forget about everything we covered in Relationships. Building trust and psychological safety are just as important, when the focus of our meetings is to move the work along and achieve results.

Most of this part of the book covers how to run meetings made up mainly of discussions. A stand-alone chapter is also dedicated to the 'workflow meeting' or update/status meeting (Chapter 30). Workflow meetings tend to take place regularly, and are more about checking in with each other than making huge leaps in the work, or generating specific outcomes. While in the colocated space they can be seen as a waste of time, when they are held online they can provide a space for team members to reconnect, as long as progress is reported in a way that is useful to the team – as opposed to listing tasks and progress status. For those teams not used to meeting online, the predictable structure and content of the workflow meeting can provide a safe space to get used to conversing online.

A chapter is also included on running hybrid meetings, where there are both colocated and remote participants. Although this set-up is far from ideal, sometimes it is unavoidable, so there are a few things you can do to make the experience more comfortable and efficient.

Regardless of your set-up and how you run your meeting, the first question should be: 'Who should be there?' And this is where the next chapter starts.

19

Who is there, and who needs to be there?

Team meetings do not require all your team members – there is such a thing as too many people attending a meeting. How many people is 'too many' will depend on what the meeting is for: there will be times when you need everyone there; but if you have a large team, consider whether everyone's presence is necessary at every meeting.

PERFECTLY SIZED TEAMS

First, a definition. A team is a group of two or more people working together on a task. Some departments call themselves 'teams', but individuals can carry out their tasks independently from each other, and often are rewarded for individual rather than team performance.

According to Richard Hackman, the late thought leader and academic in the fields of teamwork and leadership in organisations, the optimum number of members in a team is somewhere between four and six, with ten as the maximum number. As team size increases, each member devotes more time to coordination chores (and less time to doing the work), more hand-offs between the growing cast of members are required (creating opportunities for miscommunication and mistakes), and because each member must divide his or her attention among a longer list of colleagues, the team's social glue weakens (and destructive conflict soars).[57]

---

57   Richard Hackman, in Bob Sutton (2014) 'Why big teams suck: Seven (plus or minus two) is the magical number once again', *Work Matters*, 3 March. Available at: http://bobsutton. typepad.com/my_weblog/2014/03/why-big-teams-suck-seven-plus-or-minus-two-is-the-magical-number-once-again.html

Nancy Kline, in *Time to Think*, suggests that people stop feeling safe to say what they think when group size goes beyond 12.[58]

Second, the more participants there are in a meeting, the more difficult it is for everyone to participate equally. Considerate team members with a lot to say might hold back for fear of dominating the conversation; while others might be afraid of wasting people's time as they think out loud through a problem; on the flip side, some team members might want to share every single opinion. There is also a danger of people in large groups becoming guarded and less candid with each other than they would be in a small group.

Third, if we get used to light conversations in our large team, soon the difficult topics and conversations which require in-depth discussion are left completely out of team meetings, and instead are discussed at the fringes, resulting in some team members missing out on crucial conversations.

Finally, the more people present in a meeting, the more difficult it is to contribute spontaneously to the conversation. Team members begin to rely on the team leader or facilitator to bring them into the conversation, and it is easy to hold back something you wanted to say when the conversation has moved on. On video, it becomes difficult to read people's faces, as the size of the video boxes decreases when the group size increases. On audio, instead of listening to the content of the conversation, we focus on identifying those sounds signalling that someone wants to speak. We are less likely to speak out for fear of interrupting someone else.

THE RIGHT PEOPLE

If there are more than ten people in your team, being more selective about who attends might improve the quality of your meetings. For most meetings, you and your team members can ask yourselves:

- What do we want to achieve at this meeting, and who needs to be there for it to happen?
- Who will we cancel the meeting for, if they can't attend?
- Who has the most or up-to-date knowledge to contribute?

---

58   Nancy Kline (2002) *Time to Think*, Cassell Illustrated (Kindle Edition), location 738.

- Who will be impacted by what is discussed?
- Who might learn something from attending and
  taking part?[59]

On top of this, you might need to role-model a culture where it's OK to ask to join a meeting that you haven't been formally invited to, or to decline attending one that doesn't seem relevant to your work. For example, attending an online meeting just to be informed of what is going on is unnecessary, unless the information is complex and cannot be conveyed in any other way.

In addition, you can make team meetings optional. Sometimes this is controversial, as managers think: '*What if no one turns up?*' If you are thinking that optional meetings will lead to no-shows, you need to ask yourself why.

One final thing to consider: while attending a meeting on the move is now possible, it is not always desirable. I have been in meetings when people have attended from their cars, during a train journey, even while they were shopping for a gift for a colleague. This scenario is covered in Part 4: The Kit, but I wanted to raise it here too, because while accommodating people on the move can signal that you are a team comfortable with modern ways of working, and that you are so committed to the work that you will attend meetings regardless of where you are, this is not always the best option. People on the move tend to be distracted, and their context can distract others too. Far better to reschedule the meeting, or plan how the missing team member will catch up later on.

TEAMS AND SUB-TEAMS

Another option is to consider holding meetings in smaller groups. This gives individuals more opportunity to contribute to the discussion, express their opinions, discover common ground and ask for clarification when they disagree with others. Through these closer interactions individuals can realise how they add value to the team, and get to know each other better.

---

59   Adapted from Paul Axtell (2018) 'The most productive meetings have fewer than 8 people', *Harvard Business Review*, 22 June. Available at: https://hbr.org/2018/06/the-most-productive-meetings-have-fewer-than-8-people

If you have been working in an 'all-hands-on-deck' fashion that is resulting in too many meetings, it might be time for people to clarify their responsibilities and involvement in the project. In this way, you can identify which team members need to be having in-depth discussions and about what, which in turn clarifies decisions on how to form sub-teams. If you decide to experiment with meeting in smaller groups, consider how this will affect the rest of your ecosystem. Meetings are part of your overall communication practice, and if you change how you run them, you could affect other aspects of your teamwork.

If you and your team members enjoy each other's company, and that is a big part of being happy at work, the team might resist breaking out into smaller groups. In that case, consider making meetings optional, so that people can drop out when meetings are interfering with their work patterns.

A QUESTION OF TIME

Someone turning up late to a meeting online can be just as disruptive as this is to a colocated meeting. How we deal with it affects the meeting, our relationship with our team members, and the norms generated in our team. Most of the advice I have come across recommends starting on time regardless of who is present, suggesting that people turn up early to check their equipment and reminding people of the importance of good timekeeping.

I say 'Yes!' to all of that, but suggest you also consider preparing for when people are late.

Rather than be thrown off balance by late arrivals, accept that computers can crash, just as public transport can suffer delays. Agree on an easy method for people to let others know that they will be late when life gets in the way, whether through the meetings area in your collaboration platform, a chat message, email or text. Show through your behaviour that it's important to be on time:[60] if someone is going to be even just one minute late, they need to send a message.

---

60   This will be more important in some cultures than others. In new teams, it's worth stating the expectation that the meeting will start at the time for which it has been called.

If technical problems are constantly making people late, consider changing your meeting platform. You might also want to ask individuals to review their equipment, and assess whether you should find the cash to upgrade their devices or move on to a more reliable tool. Should you switch platforms, know that your first meetings in the new set-up will include some teething problems, so do bear that in mind too when you schedule meetings.

During busy times for your team or periods of change in the organisation, think about how team members will catch up if they are late to meetings. Last-minute requests from other people in the organisation or urgent troubleshooting can interfere with meeting plans. For example, you might start recording your meetings, or allocate one person at each meeting to update those who couldn't make it.

NOTICE WHAT IS HAPPENING

I am not supporting that we nurture a culture where it's absolutely fine to arrive late at meetings. Being late can be seen as a lack of respect for other people's time in many organisations. However, at this stage, I would like to quote my friend Lisette Sutherland, who suggests that when someone annoys us, we "assume positive intent". I am going to ask that you assume that nobody enjoys being late to a meeting, and so when they are, there is no point in adding to their own worries or concerns. Instead, if someone is persistently late, find out why.

Personal reasons

It could be due to personal reasons, commitment issues or the time of the day when the meeting is being held.

A waste of time

They could be making a point that meetings are a waste of time – in which case, there is a more difficult conversation to be had. See whether you can speak to the team member straight after the meeting, either by asking them to hang around or by chatting in private. Try starting the conversation with something neutral, such as: "I've noticed you're late recently to our meetings, are you having problems with the tech?"

Waiting for notifications

Another reason that people are late to online meetings more frequently than colocated ones is because they are waiting for their calendar notification to pop up. As you don't need to change location, why should you add 'travel time' or a reminder 10 minutes earlier? Find out whether the regular offenders are using last-minute notifications to jolt them into the meeting.

Acknowledge new arrivals

If you are running a meeting and someone is late, acknowledge that they have just joined you. Even when you are on video, there is a chance that not all streams might be visible to everyone. If you are working audio-only, some people might not be aware that a new person has joined the group.

Some platforms show when someone has joined the meeting through a doorbell sound or an announcement, but sometimes new people can slip in without making a sound.

. . . .

I was once meeting a client with other consultants when halfway through, I noticed that there was a name on the attendee list that I didn't recognise. I wrote in the chat:

"Who is Graham MacDonald, and why is he here in this meeting?"

Two seconds later, Graham left. I never found out who he was.

. . . .

MAKE YOUR MEETINGS MATTER

- Notice whether everyone attends all of your meetings by default. Is this important in your team? If you are a large team, are team members meeting strategically?
- Could reducing the number of times when you all meet together free up people to pursue only those meetings that are meaningful to them?

<u>20</u>

Should we meet to decide?

"So, those are our three options. Shall we think about it and then decide which one we should go for? Although I have little space in my calendar to have a meeting…"

My colleague and I were meeting with a client to come up with a few options on how to move forward with a project. We had reached the point when we needed to sleep on it, then decide which option we preferred. Unless one of us thought of a fourth option, we all disagreed or new, complex information came to light, there was no reason to meet. And yet calling a meeting was the default approach to making a decision. In some companies there is such a strong meeting culture that the option of deciding asynchronously is overlooked. When we need to make a decision, we call a meeting.

In the online space, we need to be mindful of calling too many meetings –no commuting is involved, so the effort to attend seems small; there are no rooms to be booked, so we don't have to worry about space availability. It's way too easy to call a meeting and invite people with just one click. (Imagine if you had to phone everyone you wanted to come to a meeting: would that decrease the number of meetings scheduled? Plus during your phone call, you would need to explain the reasons for attending.)

While there is value in having regular meetings with your team, as discussed throughout Part 2: Relationships, it's also important to prevent 'meeting fatigue'. Some decisions need to be made following high-quality, real-time conversations; while others only require exchanging a few messages online. Other times, you might need to have an asynchronous, lengthy conversation over a week, so that people can take time to reflect and contribute at their own pace, gathering later online to check that everyone is aligned.

DO WE REALLY NEED A MEETING?

If you are about to call a meeting to make a decision in your team, consider the following.

Overall importance

How high are the stakes? How much will the decision outcome affect you all? For how long will you have to live with it?

Complexity of the decision

How complicated or ambiguous is the situation? If it's a simple problem, such as should you invest in the paid version of your current collaboration platform, a text-based conversation might be all you need to have. Conversely, the decision to recruit a new team member will benefit from a richer conversation, where your instinct also plays a part.

Who will be affected

This question helps you decide who needs to be present. If some of your team members will be expected to use their own judgement, initiative and creativity to implement the decision, they will need to be at the meeting.

These three criteria can also help you to plan your meeting. For example, if it will be difficult to make the decision, and it will have a considerable and long-term impact on your team, you might prefer to schedule three different meetings over a week, rather than trying to squeeze it all into one session. Or perhaps after considering the criteria, you realise that although it is a low-impact, easy scenario, the outcome will affect many people. In that case, you might want to kick off an asynchronous conversation, and get team members' input over a week. Following that, you can assess whether you need a meeting to clarify any of the points made, or whether you can make a decision without gathering online.

Once you have decided that a meeting is worth your time, consider how the rest of your communication ecosystem will support it.

- How much information can you share beforehand?
- Is that information easy to access and digest?
- Are there specific things that people should look out for

when reading the information, any thoughts they could formulate?
- Can you kick off the discussion asynchronously, to surface different viewpoints before the meeting?

Sometimes, creating the agenda can lead to an asynchronous conversation that replaces the meeting – not a bad thing if you are trying to cut down on meetings.

....

INSPIRATION

Blocksparks is a distributed company that helps blockchain companies to communicate their message and develop their brand. Its team is made up of writers, so they are comfortable communicating through text. Blocksparks CEO, Maya Middlemiss, shared this anecdote with me.

> "I was getting ready for the next meeting with my two team members. As a way of gathering my thoughts, I opened a text document and started to draft the agenda.
>
> I wanted to share my thinking behind some items, giving some context around them, so that my team members could be better prepared. As I typed away, I found myself narrating my thinking, explaining my decisions and elaborating on the agenda points to such an extent that suddenly I had communicated in writing everything I needed to say at the meeting.
>
> The other team members read through my notes, commented on them, added their thoughts, and we started a quick conversation on the document. That meant that our next meeting was dedicated to a more even conversation in the team, rather than being mainly about understanding my own thinking and asking for clarification on my decisions."

....

MAKE YOUR MEETINGS MATTER

- When you meet to make a decision, does everyone have enough information to make the most out of your time together?
- Does the decision really need a meeting, or can it be made in any other way?

21

Is everyone comfortable with the tech?

I'm struggling with my team, because some are based in remote areas (really 'remote', not just connected by tech) and our meetings are quite painful. On the other hand, the CEO and the board have access to the most amazing technology so, for them, getting together is a breeze. They don't understand what we struggle with.

The above scenario shows that working with technology can cause inequality – but sometimes this is overlooked. Having better systems for some people rather than others can result in different experiences at a meeting, affecting relationships.

While I hope this example doesn't resonate with you, remember that the different ways in which you and your team members interact with technology can affect your team dynamics.

GO OVER THE BASICS

We all have a different relationship with technology. Some people are afraid of trying out new software and installing new applications, while others have been using the same applications for ages and are happy to continue using them, despite their limitations. And some of us happily experiment with a new platform, figuring out how it works on our own.

To have comfortable team meetings, all team members need to know how to use the meeting platform. Regardless of how regularly they have had online meetings in the past, we can't assume that all team members will know how to carry out simple functions, such as sharing their screen or accessing the chat facility.

If some of your team members are unfamiliar with meeting online or using your meeting platform, spend some time with them to discover and experiment with its features. Find half an hour to hop online together and go through the different functions. If one or two people are struggling more than others, spend some time with them individually, or make sure that another team member can train them to use the tool. (You could ask your IT department to do this, but you would be missing out on an opportunity to strengthen your team.)

Even if you are familiar with the application yourself, review its use every now and then. Developers change the interface or add new features regularly, so it's easy to spend months using an application before discovering its most useful features.

. . . .

I was running a training session for a group of managers, and we were discussing the extra time that it can take to communicate in a virtual team. I thought I would check whether they were familiar with the feature in their smartphones that could save them time when writing messages.

"Do you see this little microphone icon, sitting by the space bar in the keyboard? That transcribes your speech into writing."

The 15 managers sitting around the table were all ecstatic with this new discovery. The feature had been there all along, but they had never come across it. All except one: a lady who had previously expressed her concern about using so much technology to communicate with her team.

"Did you really not know about this feature?" she said. "I might not know how to use WhatsApp or Skype, but I've been using that little microphone for months!"

. . . .

THE BASICS

If you are in the early stages of running online meetings, using a new platform or have new members in your team, check that everyone knows how to:

- Turn on their microphone on and off
- Turn their camera on and off
- Change how their username appears to others (of more importance when there are new members in the team, or if you are meeting with external collaborators or clients)
- Share a screen
- Use the chat
- Hide themselves (if the platform has this feature)
- Choose how many people appear on the screen (if there is a choice)

While many people attending meetings love seeing multiple faces on their screen, there are some for whom this might be overwhelming. Make sure everyone knows how to change this, as the default option might not be the preferred one.

Default settings

Most meeting platforms have a host, the person who 'owns' the account. That might well be you, or in large corporations, is set by whoever is registered with the product. The host can turn certain features on and off, and limit what attendees can do during a meeting.

Some platforms have been built on the assumption that everyone in a meeting will want to contribute equally to it, while others have been designed assuming that one or two people will lead the session and be responsible for the content. You should know what the default settings of your platform are, understand their limitations and how they will affect your team dynamics. As much as you can, customise your platform to run meetings in the way that suits your team best.

If you are the account owner, you might want to give a couple of people (if not the whole team) hosting or admin powers to the meeting. In addition, you could ask someone else in the team to be the account owner, signalling that the responsibility to organise and run a meeting, even just at the technical level, should be shared within the team. From a practical viewpoint, having someone else with hosting powers means that if the host drops off the call, the system doesn't kick everyone out of the meeting.

Of course, these last points are relevant if you work within an organisation where the technology is controlled by someone else; but still, always aim to understand your platform's settings, and find out how you can customise it to facilitate your meetings in the most effective way.

. . . .

I once attended a meeting in an organisation where people rarely turned on their video. I hadn't met some people there, and so I thought an interaction over video would be beneficial to all.

I decided to role-model by turning on my webcam. It didn't work. Was I clicking in the wrong place? Was my camera broken?

The answer was more depressing: the administrators had disabled participants' ability to turn on their video. What I thought was a norm (an unspoken rule) had become a rule – and now, the way that the tech had been set up was limiting how people interacted online.

. . . .

MAKE YOUR MEETINGS MATTER

- Are you using your meeting platform to give you and your team members the best meeting experience?
- Are some team members' contributions being limited by their ability to use technology?

22

Agendas or points of conversation

Many moons ago, I used to run a theatre company from a little office in an arts centre in London. Every four months, we had board meetings. In my role as company secretary, every quarter I would sit behind the office computer and print off the agenda and the other papers we needed for the meeting. I laid them all out on one of our desks (we only had two), collate them, stick them in an A4 envelope, licked the stamps that went on the top right corner and finally dropped the little packages into the postbox on my way home. Anything that emerged between the time I sent off the envelopes and the meeting would be inserted into the agenda under 'A.O.B.' (Any Other Business).

Then email made its way into the world of work, and I could save on stamps and envelopes by attaching the documents to electronic messages, confirming the time and date of the meeting. Now, meeting documents don't even live on my computer anymore: they live in shared team folders, where they can be altered by anyone taking part in the meeting right up until the start time, and even during it.

You might not need an agenda for your regular or workflow meetings, if they have developed a rhythm of their own. But if you are meeting to solve a problem, review a project or make a decision, it will help to have a structure to guide you through the discussion. You can call it an 'agenda', or use more informal terms such as 'points of conversation' or 'meeting plan'. (Personally, I prefer to create 'points of conversation' rather than an 'agenda'. It reminds us that we are there to interact with each other.)

There are different ways to co-create your agenda, and you will need to pick the one that fits your team identity best. If your team meets regularly, a few bullet points on 'what we'd like to cover' might be all you need; but if your team meets only once a month, you might want to adopt a more holistic approach.

In her book, *Virtual Leadership*, Penny Pullan suggests the following headings for a team meeting:

1. We are here to… – clarifies the purpose. What is the meeting for?
2. Today we will… – specifies the objectives of the meeting, what will be the outcomes?
3. Our plan – how long will each item need?
4. Who is doing what – what role will different people take? (See Chapter 10)
5. How we work together – how will you signal you want to speak, etc.? (See Chapter 4)
6. What's next – who will do what, next?[61]

If you agree on points 1–5 before the meeting starts, once you gather online you will be ready to go straight into the conversation. The best way of laying down your meeting plan is by putting your thoughts together in a document in the cloud.

THE CLOUD

Co-creating the agenda can take place in a shared document in the cloud, in parallel to your everyday work.

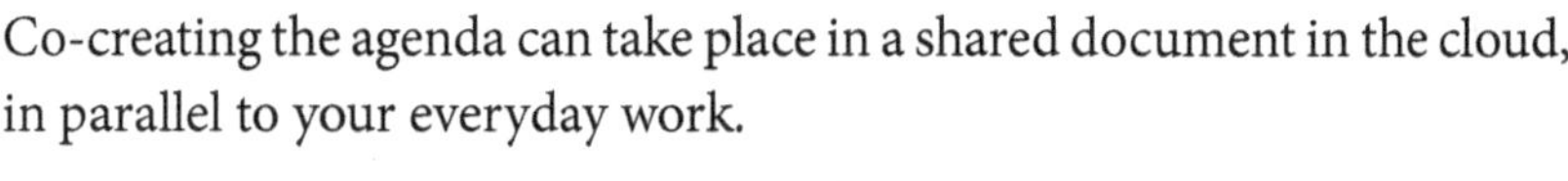

INSPIRATION

The five-person management team at TimeDoctor, a company producing time-tracking software, holds weekly meetings. Most of the leadership teams' information-sharing and discussion takes place when they gather online in real time.

During the week, individuals add items to the agenda as they come up in their workflow. In this way, no one has to worry about

---

61 Penny Pullan (2016), *Virtual Leadership: Practical Strategies for Getting the Best Out of Virtual Work Teams*, Kogan Page.

creating and circulating the agenda: it is always ready in the cloud for them.[62] The meeting plan builds itself up during the week, and is ready in time for the meeting.

. . . .

There is another benefit to co-creating agendas. At Convert.com, putting together the meeting plan has resulted sometimes in questions being answered before the meeting itself.[63] One or two comments in the shared document have saved team members minutes of discussion. A great example of integrating asynchronous communication systems with meeting plans.

Putting together an agenda so that anyone in the team can annotate and modify it, can create a sense of shared ownership of the meeting. With communication systems that allow us to share and update documents quickly, there is no need for a manager to create the agenda on their own or be responsible for distributing it. Co-creating agendas is a way of signalling to team members that it is for them to make the most out of the meeting.

STRUCTURING THE AGENDA

For simple meetings, your agenda could consist of a list of topics. At the beginning of the meeting, have a quick discussion to agree on the order in which to cover each item, then adjust the document accordingly. For more complex meetings, set a deadline by which everyone can suggest topics and questions, to give you enough time to structure the agenda beforehand.

When you are finalising your meeting plan, resist the temptation to put all the 'easy items' at the beginning.[64] Use the time when everyone is focused and energised to discuss those issues important to you, those that are difficult. The last thing you want is to run out of time before you

---

62   Interview with Rob Rawson, CEO of TimeDoctor, in Virtual Not Distant (2018) 'WLP162: Should we be tracking people's time?', podcast, 22 March. Available at: www. virtualnotdistant.com/podcasts/time-tracking

63   Personal communication (conversation) with Morgan Legge, 2017.

64   Eric J. McNulty (2017) 'How to maximize meetings', *Strategy + Business*, 10 July. Available at: www.strategy-business.com/blog/How-to-Maximize-Meetings

discuss that one crucial issue that everyone has been waiting for, or to finally get to it when everyone is suffering from virtual fatigue.

Live agenda creation

A common objection that employees have to meeting regularly is that meetings can interrupt an individual's workflow. Often, what takes place in meetings is unconnected to the work they have been carrying out moments before they start.

If this is the case in your team, consider creating the agenda at the beginning of your meeting, rather than in advance. In this way, team members can bring up whatever is of more urgency or importance to them at the time. While creating the agenda can be seen as a time expense, focusing the meeting on what is on people's minds can incorporate them into their work.

Points of conversation can be created by jotting down what those present would like to talk about on a spreadsheet, Kanban board (see below), sticky note canvas or another tool designed for this purpose. (How to create an agenda with a slides tool is also discussed below.) Once the suggestions are shared, you can create the agenda by prioritising the most popular or time-sensitive items.

An alternative plan

If you are having a one-item meeting, or have decided not to use an agenda, you might want to open with: "What would you like to get from this meeting?"

This is how Judy Rees, co-author of *Clean Language: Revealing Metaphors and Opening Minds* and remote collaboration consultant, starts many meetings. While it might not be appropriate for your general catch-ups or those meetings with a packed agenda, this question can be great for focusing everyone's minds on the meeting, reminding them to take an active role. In addition, it can align everyone's expectations of what needs to be discussed (and gives everyone the opportunity to speak at the beginning of the meeting).

MEETING WITH PEOPLE OUTSIDE YOUR TEAM

If you are meeting with others outside your team or even your organisation – especially if you rarely meet with them – make sure you have a solid framework for discussions. When we don't know others, it is tricky to negotiate the tempo of a meeting and balance discussion with planning for action.

When norms emerge around how meetings are run, it is easy to forget that there are other ways to gather online. If you are meeting with people outside your team, check whether they want to use video, and whether they will share documents online with you.

It's also worth doing a bit of housekeeping, making sure your name is turning up as you want it to on the platform. If a few team members are attending the meeting, consider adding your role in the team or organisation to your name. If you are not using video, but the platform enables you to upload a profile picture, do so.

Regarding content, there is plenty that can be borrowed from the colocated space:

- Include timings with topics of discussion to help the meeting end on time.
- Find out what the expectations are around meetings from the people outside your team:
  - Do they always meet with an agenda?
  - Do they need to have it a few days in advance?
  - Are they all right with just turning up?

In their book *Kill Bad Meetings*, the authors quote a project manager in a technology company in Germany, saying that in their organisation, 'if an agenda for a regular meeting has not been circulated seven days before the meeting, it is automatically cancelled'.[65]

As you and your team get used to meeting together, you are likely to build assumptions about how meetings should be run. Don't assume that all other teams and individuals will run their meetings in the same way.

---

65   Kevan Hall and Alan Hall (2017) *Kill Bad Meetings*, Nicholas Brealey Publishing (Kindle Edition), location 829.

USING ONLINE TOOLS TO VISUALISE YOUR AGENDA

An agenda doesn't have to consist of a list of bullet points. An online tool that allows you to move tasks or items around, where you can tick off what you have already discussed, might be more useful and fun to use. (I know, who thought working through an agenda could be fun!)

Using Kanban board-style tools

Personally, I find online tools set up as Kanban boards to be the most useful. It is a scheduling system developed at Toyota to make supply chain management more efficient. This system has been broadly adopted to help teams visualise their workflow: it's a quick way of knowing what work is being carried out in the team, and at what stage of completion each task is. Kanban boards are used to communicate status, progress and issues during the product development process. Each issue or item is written on one sticky note or card, which is moved across the board as the work progresses. Tasks are moved from areas labelled 'Working On' to 'Completed', for example; or from 'In Preparation' to 'This Week'.

When preparing a meeting, you can place all the items you want to discuss in one area of the tool: for example, labelled 'For Discussion'. As the items are discussed, you can move them to another area, such as 'Done' or 'For Next Meeting'. In this way, everyone can visualise the flow of the meeting. (For more on this, see Chapter 30.)

Using slides to co-create your agenda

A shared slide tool can come in handy for this. Each slide contains one agenda item, and you move the slides around to create a plan. Just make notes on each slide as you go along, so that at the end of the meeting, *voilà!* – there are your meeting notes.

Imagine you are holding a mid-project meeting. As the date draws near, you all start thinking individually about those things you need to share, learn more about or troubleshoot. You pop into the agenda document and add a slide for the item you would like to incorporate into your agenda. The content can be a screenshot, image, shape, colour or words.

Once everyone has added their contribution, you can move the slides around to create your meeting plan – which is a collection of different visual stimuli.

Warning!

Having meetings on your computer, where you have immediate access to other tools and the internet, can be dangerous.

If you are a 'tool junkie', you will love the fact that this book is encouraging you to use different tools to create your agenda. Your imagination might be running wild with all the other kinds of tools you could be using during meetings. Be careful: you might be in danger of putting tools centre stage, and increasing the chances of your meetings being unproductive and clunky.

MAKE YOUR MEETINGS MATTER

- Which of your meetings need tight agendas, and which could benefit from a looser structure?
- Are you planning meeting content to best suit the aim, timing and people attending?

23

Taking notes and recording meetings

When I first started attending committee meetings, way back in my early twenties, I used to jot down every single discussion and created heavy, thorough minutes. Reading them was like watching a soap opera: they included every bit of conversation, even those that went nowhere. Now I rarely come across anything resembling minutes, just follow-up action and decision points.

If you are taking minutes at your meeting, ask yourself why. There might be other ways of capturing key decisions and summarising the meeting for those not present.

CAPTURING IMPORTANT INFORMATION

Jotting down action points

A document with meeting notes might not be the best place to see your pending actions or tasks. Most likely you will only get round to looking at them just before your next meeting, when you look back at the notes.

It's better to put your action points straight into your project management tool or other shared platform, where you visualise your workflow.

Recording a decision

Are you doing this for accountability? To have a formal record of decision-making? Or to make a note of those actions that need to be taken? In which case, what sort of action, by whom and when? Is there a more visible place to include them in your ecosystem, one that you all use regularly?

Sometimes we take meeting notes as a way of committing to a course of action and clarifying what we need to tackle next. If those notes aren't revisited or don't make their way into our everyday online communication, they are useless. What is worse, those notes can be interpreted as a lack of accountability or interest – just one more list of things we said we would do at the meeting, but never got around to doing.

Another way of capturing what has happened at a meeting is to record it. Let's quickly review some of what we covered in Chapter 12.

Note-taking for non-attendees

Are you recording for those who weren't present at the meeting? Fair enough, that is probably the best reason for doing this at all.

RECORDING YOUR MEETINGS

One advantage that online meetings have over their colocated counterparts is that we can record them. This is useful if one or two team members can't be at the meeting and really need to be involved in the conversation. A recording can be useful also for those who feel that they don't need to contribute to the conversation, but would still like to understand how decisions came about.

Lisette Sutherland, creator of 'Collaboration Supercards'[66] has even created a card saying 'Shall we record this meeting?', as a playful way to check visually whether it's OK to record.

If you do record your meetings, and are all working from a document or referring to a website during the conversation, use screen-sharing so that the people watching can see what you are looking at as well. Alternatively, make sure that when you post the link to the recording, you add a note that says something like: "We referred to these documents during the meeting, here are the links."

If you have agreed that the people watching the recording will take part in the conversations that emerged during the meeting, make sure there is a space to do this online, and that their contributions are acknowledged.

Warning!

While recording your meetings might seem like a productive idea, it could be disastrous for psychological safety. The meetings we are more likely

---

66   Collaboration Supercards are cards that help participants to communicate visually with
      each other during online meetings: www.collaborationsuperpowers.com/supercards/

to record are those involving strategy or decision-making, and require open discussion (see Chapter 8).

Think about it: in deep discussion, we are being encouraged to share our thoughts, reactions, even feelings, all the while being recorded for posterity. Plus, regularly having a recording for later viewing might mean that we start to undervalue real-time conversations and presence.

We want to avoid thinking: '*I don't feel like attending, and there will be a recording anyway*', rather than: '*Such a shame I can't make it. Oh well, at least I can catch up with the recording.*'

I have seen this happen in online communities, where people ask whether an interactive session or meeting will be recorded. This turns experiences and opportunities for human interaction into broadcasts and displays of behaviour. Make recording the exception, rather than the rule.

MAKE YOUR MEETINGS MATTER

- Are you creating extra work for yourself by taking notes during meetings, or is it really necessary?
- What is the best way to capture what happened in the meeting, so that it can be easily accessible after the fact?

<u>24</u>

Kicking off the meeting

Your tech is ready and you have your plan. It's time to start the meeting.

Turning up 10 minutes early to an online meeting can help us leave our other work behind. It also gives us the opportunity to chat casually to anyone else who has arrived beforehand. In busy teams, this can be the only time when people feel relaxed enough to connect as individuals, and share what is going on in their minds (or their lives outside work).

The only drawback is that if you have a team that easily moves into informal chatter, it's difficult to stop the conversation. Kicking off the meeting formally with something like "Shall we get going?" shifts things on to business. Don't be afraid to cut through the conversations that will have started between those arriving early. Side conversations are difficult to cut off in the online space because, for example, Fred and Louise can't talk to each other without everyone else hearing and being involved.[67]

If you are someone who enjoys banter and usually ends up having those side conversations yourself, make sure it isn't you who is holding everyone up.

WHO IS HERE?

Use the first couple of minutes in the meeting to give everyone the chance to speak. There is a practical reason for this, as mentioned previously: if there is a problem with the technology or internet connection, it's better to find out before the conversation gets going rather than in the middle of it.

---

67   At the time of writing, there is no way of having a side conversation with one person (unless you use the chat function) without everyone else being involved; however, the technology to enable this might well be around the corner.

. . . .

INSPIRATION

There is also a psychological benefit to speaking to the group at the beginning of a meeting. In 2014, the World Health Organization introduced the 'Surgery Safety Checklist': a tool to improve the safety of surgical procedures by involving the whole surgery team in safety checks at the start of the operation. The first item in the checklist, before skin incision, asks that all team members introduce themselves by name and role:

> Even if everyone knows each other, introductions are important as they reinforce team communication. An important part of the introductions is to enable every member of the team to speak aloud when they introduce themselves. There is evidence that once an individual has spoken aloud once they will be more likely to speak up again if they have concerns later. This is particularly important for junior team members.[68]

. . . .

FIRST WORDS

Unless you are a new team, there won't be a need for you to introduce each other; but a quick catch-up on how your day has been or how you are feeling might be appropriate. These first words also present an opportunity to 'work out loud' by sharing something that has happened or you have achieved, which might interest other team members. It is also a way of reminding yourselves that the work you do as individuals can be of use to others in the team.

Moreover, taking turns to speak can set the tone of a meeting. It's worth finding a balance between always checking in via the same way (which builds a sense of ritual and team identity), and varying how you kick off the meeting, so that answers don't become routine and meaningless.

In addition to the questions outlined in Chapter 7 ('Should We Talk about the Weather?'), here is a set of 'round robin' instructions designed

---

68   World Health Organization (2014) 'Safe surgery saves lives: Frequently asked questions', August. Available at: www.who.int/patientsafety/safesurgery/faq_introduction/en/

to start a meeting on a positive note[69] while also conveying information about the work:

- Name one thing you have accomplished over the last few days, that you are proud of.
- Name a person who has helped you recently.
- Mention one thing you are looking forward to in the coming week/month.
- Mention something interesting you have learned in the last few days.

And though not always related to work:

- What's the funniest thing someone has told you recently?

For regular meetings, you can develop questions that only require a one-word answer, making the experience more of a 'roll call' and using it just to confirm that everyone is present in both mind and (virtual) body.

Once everyone has spoken at least once, check that the tech is ready and everyone has access to the tools and/or documents needed for the meeting. If you have called the meeting for a specific purpose, recap it and ask whether anyone is expecting something different – it's much better to find this out right at the start, than two minutes before the meeting ends.

OPERATING IN A BUSY WORLD

If your team is going through a difficult or busy time, you might want to start the meeting with individuals sharing what is on their mind, or what might be happening in your surroundings which can distract you from the meeting. Perhaps, for example, Louise has a piece of work that she needs to complete by the end of the day; or there could be a heated conversation taking place behind Fred that is distracting his attention (Figure 9).

---

69   Alexander (2007) 'Five weeeeeeeeird tips for great meetings', *The Chief Happiness Officer Blog*, 20 February. Available at: https://positivesharing.com/2007/02/five-weeeeeeeeird-tips-for-great-meetings/

Figure 9: Behind the camera

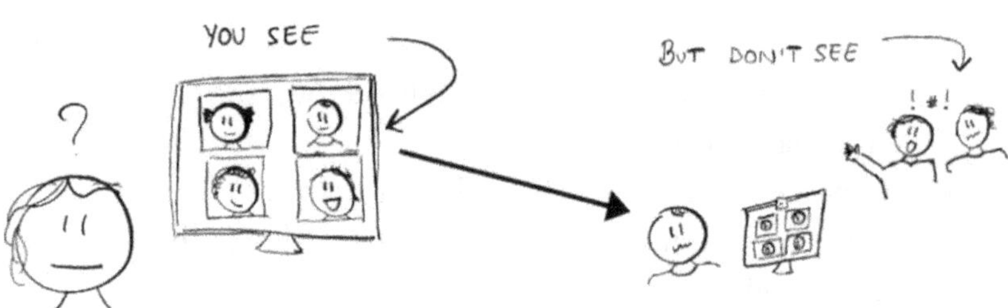

By sharing what is on their mind, the individual has the chance to 'dump' that information out of their head and into the group, helping them to concentrate on the meeting. At the same time, the rest of the team can avoid wondering why on earth Fred looks so distracted today.

A quiet start

How about starting the meeting in silence? You and your team members can review the documents or information needed for the meeting, read through the agenda or think through what you want to get from the session. Although we think of our time together as a time of ongoing interaction, creating this reflective space signals the importance of being ready before we start the discussion.

When using video, having your webcams on during this personal time tunes you into the team; when using audio, leave your microphones unmuted, to get used to listening to the team's silence.

If wellbeing plays an important part in your value system, consider starting your meetings with mindfulness practice.

Whenever we schedule reflective time for ourselves as individuals or as a team, it can be reduced to make room for urgent tasks or conversations. Creating the space at the beginning of the meeting for everyone to take a breath, pause, focus and become truly present, could be valuable and result in a more productive meeting.

MAKE YOUR MEETINGS MATTER

- There is more than one way to start a meeting.
- Consider the nature and timing of each meeting when planning the first five minutes.

25

Screen-sharing

When online meetings became common, they frequently involved some kind of slide deck or other shared document, mainly because most conversations took place over audio. Having a shared document to look at makes for a better experience than looking at a grey meeting platform or a black box on your screen. Now that using video is more popular, there is no longer an expectation that we need anything else to look at apart from our good selves; but sharing documents on our screens does still have a place.

For example, if you are talking through a budget, you can pull it up on your computer and share your screen to guide others through the figures. Or if you have found something on the internet that you want to use for inspiration for a design, screen-sharing is the fastest way of showing your team members.

When using a project management tool or document as an agenda, one of you can share the screen so that the rest of the team doesn't need to shift between windows or browsers. Screen-sharing is particularly useful if there are people attending the meeting from their smartphone, or other devices with small screens.

TO SHARE, OR NOT TO SHARE?

When you need to work together on a document, make sure it is accessible to everyone before the meeting. Encourage people to pull it up at their end, rather than relying on the person leading the conversation to navigate them through the document. In this way, team members take responsibility for following the document during the conversation. Having said that, there might be times when it is more relevant and productive for one person to guide everyone else through the document through screen-sharing. Think about what will result in a better conversation.

If you are using live documents during your meeting, agree beforehand whether they should be edited during the session, and by whom. (I have been in a few meetings where I started to edit a sentence in a document, only to find that someone else was simultaneously adding the same comment a few lines below.) Decide who will edit the document during the meeting, or how you will let others know that you are about to edit it.[70]

If everyone has access to the document and is on video, be prepared for people to look distracted every now and then, as their eyes move from one part of the screen to the other.

Sharing slides

Usually, slides are used to share ideas through graphics or present data. But there are more informal ways in which you can use them. For example, if you have designed a process or plan and want to share it with your team, you can use one slide to illustrate each step and walk others through the different stages. You need not spend a lot of time on designing the slides – one word per slide will do.

Sketch it out

Whiteboards or online drawing boards come in handy to sketch our thoughts as they emerge in a meeting. Some meeting tools will have a whiteboard built into them; otherwise, you might need a separate application and ideally, a separate device such as a tablet.

---

70 Watching someone else share their screen, I have found myself instinctively reaching for the mouse and trying to scroll through the document or trying to edit it, only to realise that I was trying to click on someone else's document.

Here's the proof:

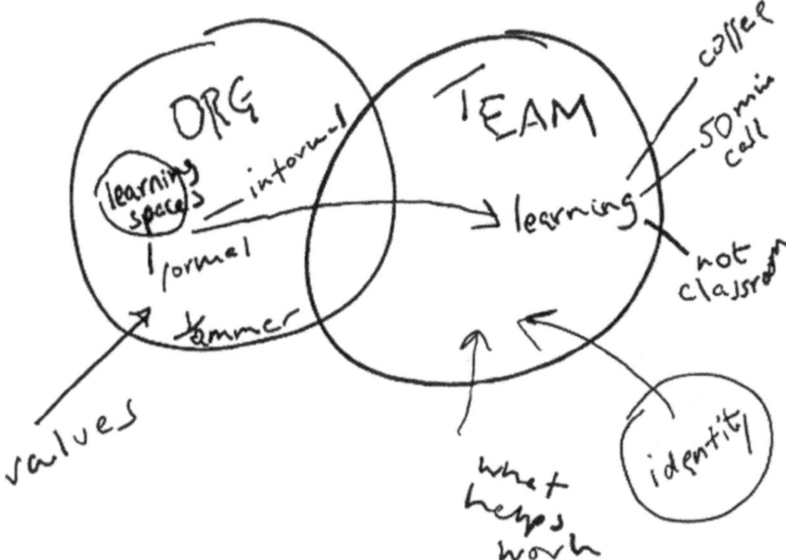

I sketched this during a conversation with a client, talking about how to identify ways of maintaining a sense of belonging in a company by introducing the opportunity to work from anywhere. As I jotted down our ideas visually, it became clear that we needed different strategies at the team and organisational levels, but there would be overlap in the activities we set up.

Creating the sketch as ideas emerged gave us a way of talking about aspects that we were not clear about. For example, "When you were talking about that stuff there, bottom-right…"

Needless to say, there was a high degree of trust in that meeting, and later I converted the sketch into a proper graphic; but you can see how sketching out my thoughts saved time and gave us clarity.

. . . .

STICK WITH IT

A few days later, I was recording a podcast episode with Penny Pullan, author of *Virtual Leadership*, who is known for using drawings and sketches during her online and offline presentations and meetings.

While talking about engaging people in online meetings, she mentioned the use of visual elements and drawing. I jumped at the opportunity to get some free advice (a perk of hosting a podcast!): "Penny, I tried using one of those sketchpads the other day, but I found it difficult to use the pen, and the results were pretty close to disastrous. Isn't it just hard to use those pens?"

Penny replied: "Don't use your mouse or your touch pad for three days, only use the tablet and pen. So three days solid, and after that you'll be fine."[71]

. . . .

If part of your work is to innovate as a team or individually, or you have meetings where you share complex ideas or concepts, it is worth investing time in learning how to use software that allows you to capture and share your ideas in different ways, not just via text. You might also want to learn to use collaborative mind-mapping software, where you can co-create diagrams and mind maps. Remember: these programmes take time to master, so make sure everyone is comfortable with the tool before you integrate it into your meetings.

No whiteboard? Go old school!

Maybe you are like me and don't have enough desk space to fit in a tablet that allows you to sketch online; or maybe you have a long list of new skills that you need to gain, and learning how to use a digital pen is by no means a priority. This doesn't mean that you can't sketch your ideas or share quick drawings or illustrations with others online: just use a good old-fashioned pen or pencil and paper.

---

71   If you want to listen to our original chat, check out Virtual Not Distant (2018) 'WLP161: Virtual leadership in project teams', podcast, 15 March. Available at: www.virtualnotdistant. com/podcasts/virtual-leadership-penny

There is nothing wrong with sketching out your thoughts on a piece of paper and holding it up to the camera, or taking a picture with your phone and uploading it where others can view it. Without going full-on with your whiteboard, you can still use it at the point of collaboration. Use a picture of your paper sketch as a starting point, then upload it to the whiteboard where other people can annotate and build on it. When you don't have the latest online tool to hand (or you don't know how to use it), just get creative with what you have. Sometimes pen and paper is the best technology available.

Use in moderation

As mentioned previously, in most meeting platforms when you share your screen, everyone's video boxes (and therefore their faces) get smaller, so look out for those moments when you should stop sharing to make their faces more visible.

If you start the meeting by screen-sharing the agenda, once you move on to your first discussion, stop sharing the document. Switching screen-sharing on and off can help to shift the feel of the meeting. Some conversations will benefit from everyone focusing on an image, some lines of text or a diagram; while others will flow better when everyone can see each other's faces. Notice how sharing a document changes the atmosphere of the meeting.

When someone is sharing the document guiding the discussion (for example, via a sticky notes board, project management tool or spreadsheet), that person ends up directing everyone's attention. This can be useful, focusing everyone on the relevant part of the document; or not, by spreading one person's tunnel vision throughout the team.

MAKE YOUR MEETINGS MATTER

- Which kinds of meetings will benefit most from having visual components?
- Do all your team members know how to share their screens, and are they aware of how to use them to make their contributions more impactful?

26

Don't speak unless you can improve the silence

When we are meeting over video, with a group of faces staring at us from our screen and a webcam pointing directly at our face, silence can be uncomfortable. In an audio meeting, silence can make us feel like communication is breaking down, like people have lost interest, as if they have gone to grab a coffee without letting us know.

If you are someone who likes to make people feel comfortable, you might be tempted to break the silence to avoid discomfort, rather than to add value to the conversation. Stop yourself.

That silence could be just what team members need to raise a difficult issue, shift to another topic or to decide that the meeting has ended. Or it might be when the most reflective of your team members collects their thoughts and shares them with the group.

THE SOUND OF THAT SAME VOICE

As in colocated meetings, there is usually one team member who contributes more than others in a discussion. They are the person who breaks the silence before others have had a chance to express themselves.

If you find that discussions tend to be dominated by one or two people, structure your meetings in such a way for others to contribute. Using silence deliberately to create thinking space, as described below, and asking someone who hasn't spoken much to kick off the conversation after the silence, is one way of evening out the discussion.

Before you ask for answers to a question or for people's opinions, another way of doing this is to say: "I'd quite like to hear from everyone, so could we go in order of how names coming up in the chat? If you have nothing to say, that's fine, just say so."

THINKING IN SILENCE

Picture this: you and your team are having a discussion, trying to figure out why you could not deliver your copy for the new website on time, which delayed its launch and really annoyed other teams in the organisation. You want to make sure that this doesn't happen again.

Michael has made the point, for the third time, that he has already suggested hiring a freelancer to help. Laura is convinced it's the online tool that you share your workflow through which let you down. Meanwhile, you want to gather information as to where communication has broken down between your team and the others. Throughout the discussion, Tony and Sam agree with everything that is being said.

At times like these, when people start repeating themselves, pause the discussion and collect your thoughts.

Two minutes of silence

When a conversation is going nowhere, it can be tempting to wrap up at a random point or leave the conversation for another time.

However, before moving on, it's worth creating the space for individuals to stop and reflect. This gives a sense of closure on the topic, rather than moving it to one side, which might close the discussion organically.

Ask team members to pause and think about what they have heard others say, and to reflect on whether some facts are missing and anyone might be jumping to conclusions. Then announce two minutes of silence. Turn off your webcam if it helps you feel more comfortable, and mute yourselves if you are likely to start typing.

The chances are that the conversation will slow down after the silence – although you also should be prepared for the conversation to get heated, as new insights emerge. There is no way of predicting what will happen, but silence will give you all the chance to stop and think for yourselves, rather than be carried away by the group's energy. This particularly helps those who need reflection time before contributing meaningfully to a discussion.

Silence before making decisions

If you are a team which has lively discussions (people talk fast, it's difficult to get a word in edgeways, the conversation is all over the place), consider introducing two minutes of silence at certain points in the meeting.

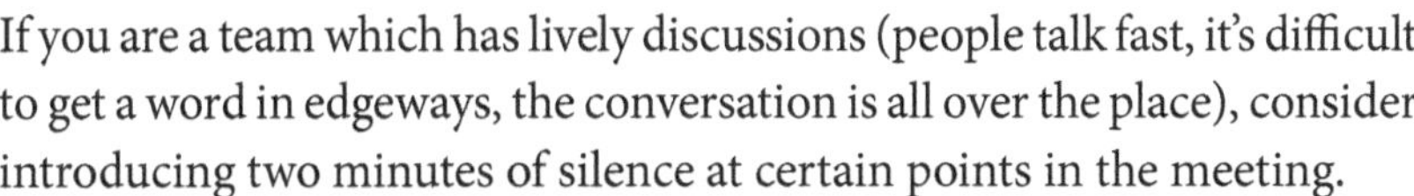

INSPIRATION

Alexander Kjerulf, founder and Chief Happiness Officer at Woohoo Inc., suggests integrating silence into discussions where you need to arrive at a decision:[72]

When discussing an issue, focus first on presenting the facts without discussing solutions. Have two minutes' silence, then discuss the options.

If discussions become heated and no progress is being made, two minutes' silence can cool the whole thing down.

When a decision has been made, give people two minutes' silence to think about how they feel about the decision.

72   Direct quote from Alexander (2007) 'Five weeeeeeeeird tips for great meetings', The Chief
      Happiness Officer Blog, 20 February. Available at: https://positivesharing.com/2007/02/five-
      weeeeeeeeird-tips-for-great-meetings/

I can hear some of you muttering to yourselves, '*Well, that's just added six more minutes to the meeting!*' Well, yes. But think about the time it might save you later on. Sometimes when people are heavily involved in a discussion, enjoying bouncing ideas off each other, they might agree to a decision in the heat of the moment without thinking through it first.

As soon as they have logged off from the meeting and got up to stretch their legs, they realise that something wasn't clear, or something that someone had said made little sense, or they remember that there was something they wanted to say that didn't find its way into the conversation – so they go back into the online team space and write: "Mmmm, I know I said I agreed, but…" Or perhaps they realise that they felt under pressure to agree with everyone else at the time. As they have no one to hand to have a quick word with, they squash their doubts and begin to care a little less about the team and the work.

Respect the silence

Silence can be uncomfortable in a meeting, but sometimes it's necessary. There might be times when you need individuals to come up with new ideas, or design the next steps for a complex project. In these cases, it is worth giving individuals time to gather their thoughts before sharing them.

Consider sharing your ideas in an online document or sticky notes board before you start the discussion, and give people time to read everyone else's comments in silence.

It's important that everyone respects the silence, and that it is not broken by those who easily get distracted by what others are writing. It will be difficult for some people to concentrate and make notes while someone else is speaking to the group, or sending a private message in the chat box.

Silence in the audio-only environment

In a meeting where we can see everyone's faces – even when we can see the whole of their bodies – sometimes it can be difficult to sense whether someone disagrees with us, unless they speak up.

There are many reasons why people might not disagree with a decision or statement made by colleagues or their manager, for fear of not being a 'team player', unconditional respect for authority, and so on. While we can't attempt to solve all those issues (and it is beyond the scope of this book to begin tackling those aspects of human behaviour), we can look out for those times when we need to prompt people to express their disagreement.

Some teams might have developed the norm of silence as a sign of agreement. (I have found this to be common.) A simple reminder of the need to verbalise agreement online can be enough to change this norm. And don't forget to thank those who make the effort!

. . . .

A group I once worked with comes to mind. After I asked questions such as "Would anyone like me to go through that again?", they would verbalise a reply only if they wanted me to repeat or clarify something.

Only after telling them a couple of times that I couldn't take silence as an affirmation, did they stop being quiet when they were happy for me to continue.

. . . .

If you have a chat facility in your meeting platform, you can ask people to type their support for an idea, disagreement or concerns. Once someone has typed "I don't agree", it's easier to invite them to express why orally. Ask people to type their opinion in the chat, but guide them to elaborate in speech, as it's much faster to explain things vocally.

If you are a new team, or if your organisation has a culture of not speaking up, you might want to frame these practices as experiments before introducing them.

When holding your meeting over audio-only, keep an ear out in case someone is quiet for a long while. Keep a list of people's names by your side, and make a note of how frequently they speak. In addition to helping you judge whether the conversation is being dominated by certain individuals, there are practical reasons for checking if someone has been quiet for too long: you never know when someone's connection has dropped off, or if their headset has stopped working.

Tech silence

There is one other type of silence in online meetings which you don't get in the colocated space: when the internet connection drops off. Even on video, when people sit still and quiet, if their image becomes 'frozen' we might not realise they have dropped off until we ask them a question directly.

Look out for these glitches, especially if you are working with new team members and are still unfamiliar with their behaviour online.

THE CULTURAL DIMENSION

In her article 'Great global meetings: Navigating cultural differences',[73] Nancy Settle-Murphy points out that silence means different things in different cultures. For example, while in some countries silence can mean that everything has been understood, in other countries it signals that people are still digesting information and thinking about what has been said. Problems start when someone shows their disagreement by being quiet, and others interpret that silence as everything being OK.

If you are still getting to know your team members, don't hesitate to ask: "I'm not sure whether the silence means anything other than you have nothing more to add. Is there something different going on in anyone's mind?"

MAKE YOUR MEETINGS MATTER

- At your next meeting, notice what happens when people are silent – and how often this happens.
- Be particularly aware of your own comfort level with silence, and consider using it regularly in your meetings to provide space for those needing reflection time.

73　Nancy Settle-Murphy (2019) 'Great global meetings: Navigating cultural differences', *InfoQ*, 30 August. Available at: www.infoq.com/articles/navigating-cultural-differences/

27

When you disagree

Meetings that matter will include disagreements. If your team members never disagree with each other, you have a problem: people might not care enough to disagree, they might be afraid to speak up; or you might have a severe case of silo mentality or 'groupthink', where people avoid disagreeing with others to preserve harmony.

During disagreements and arguments, the tempo of the discussion might speed up and different people speak – or want to speak – at the same time. If this happens, call a time out and explain why it might be necessary to structure the conversation. Remind team members that in the online space, it's difficult for organic to-and-fro conversations to work. Make it clear that you are not trying to diffuse disagreement or take control of the discussion; rather, you just want to make sure that everyone is heard and understood.

Consider using a facilitation technique called 'stacking':

- Create an order for people to speak – preferably in the order in which they are attempting to speak
- Communicate the order – perhaps by writing their names in the chat
- Ask everyone to make clear when they have finished talking, so that the next person can start.

GOING AROUND IN CIRCLES

If a disagreement is leading nowhere (that is, people can't see each other's viewpoint, and the same comments are being repeatedly made), ask whether it is OK to move the conversation to another time. Identify who needs or wants to be part of the conversation, and whether they want to continue the discussion synchronously or asynchronously. Make sure those involved set a time for the conversation to continue – ideally, straight after the meeting, or when new information emerges. It should be clear that the conversation is not being postponed to avoid disagreement, but to create the space for disagreement to lead to a useful outcome.

If the discussion is deferred, make sure that everyone present at the meeting can find out about the outcome, especially if a decision will be made during the conversation. This gives the team a sense of closure and prevents people from wondering: '*Whatever happened there?*'

Above all, don't give the impression that the team should not disagree in public – especially if the disagreement involves you, the manager. Disagreements are part of teamwork and they can be useful, but they should lead to action.

What happens in meetings will affect your other teamwork. If people begin to feel like they can't disagree with each other, they will stop disagreeing during asynchronous communication too, and the quality of the work will suffer.

. . . .

INSPIRATION

In *It Doesn't Have to Be Crazy at Work*, the founders of Basecamp explain why *they have adopted* the practice of 'disagreeing but committing':

> Good decisions [...] are always going to be the product of consultation, evidence, arguments and debate. But the only sustainable method in business is to have them made by individuals. Someone in charge has to make the final call, even if others would prefer a different decision.

Notice that the authors outline the process of consultation and debate as part of the decision-making process, but they acknowledge that sometimes a decision needs to be made so that the work can move forward. They also highlight the importance of everyone involved (that is, everyone who needs to commit to the decision) being fully aware why the decision has been made. "It's not just decide and go, it's decide, explain and go."[74]

USING BREAKOUT ROOMS

Breakout rooms allow you to form smaller groups to solve different problems in parallel, pursuing different objectives and even coming up with specific proposals which then can be presented to the whole team. It can potentially speed up the decision-making process.

'Disagreeing but committing' might be a useful strategy to adopt in some situations, but when you want to make a decision as a team, consider breaking yourself up into smaller groups to continue the discussion.

Perhaps everyone who shares a point of view can gather for 15 minutes to outline a clear, concise proposal to the rest of the group. Or there may be some benefit in putting together those with different opinions in a small group, where they have the time to express themselves slowly and ask questions to understand each other's viewpoint.

Some online platforms have breakout rooms built into them. If yours doesn't, give some thought to how you might set up parallel meetings. Set some time with your team to experiment with the system, so you don't end up figuring out how to break into smaller groups in the middle of a difficult discussion.

Turn the fact that you are meeting online into an advantage – it's much easier to set up extra meeting rooms online than it is to find them in an office building!

TAKE A TEMPERATURE CHECK

If a discussion becomes emotional or there is information overload, it might be beneficial to stop halfway through and take a 'temperature check' (you can even include this in your meeting plan).

---

74   Jason Fried and David Heinemeier Hansson (2018) *It Doesn't Have to Be Crazy at Work*, HarperCollins (Kindle Edition), location 1180.

My favourite way of checking in with others during an audio-only meeting is to ask: "What is your face doing right now?"

Sometimes, describing our physical appearance than our emotional state is easier. Similarly, over video I prefer to ask: "If you were an emoji, what kind would you be right now?" It can be less difficult to say: "I'm the purple face with the devil grin", than "I'm really cheesed off with everyone right now."

If your platform has a collection of emojis, you could use those in the chat instead; but a verbal temperature check gives everyone a chance to speak to the group directly, and reconnect.

What's under the surface?

Taking a temperature check can uncover information about people's states of mind. For example, one of your team members might look distracted during a video meeting, giving the impression that they are not interested in the conversation. However, during the temperature check they surprise you by saying something like: "My emoji would be the one that's thinking. I'm gathering all this information and trying to make sense of it, that's where I am right now."

Or someone who you thought was happy with how the discussion was going because they had been verbally agreeing might say: "My emoji is the one yawning – haven't we been through all this before?" You can't always interpret others' behaviour correctly, especially early on in your team's life.

Besides checking in with how people are feeling, your team can quickly review how the meeting is going by answering these questions halfway through:

- What is going well in this meeting, and what needs to change?
- In one sentence, what would you say this meeting is about?

Pausing to check how the meeting is going for everyone can help you decide whether to change direction, or to continue on the same track.

BRING IN THE CONTEXT

While we are having a meeting, life goes on around us.

. . . .

One winter not too long ago, when snowstorms were disrupting travel in the UK, I was leading an in-person workshop in Scotland. Just before we broke for lunch, I took a temperature check. The first person to speak up was a manager who had been called out of the room earlier by a colleague. He said:

> My emoji looks incredibly worried. What's going around my head right now is that the terrible weather is fast approaching, and we have a conference planned for tomorrow. I'm worried that we will have several people stranded here, unable to get home if the snow continues. So my mind right now is on deciding whether we should cancel the event.

His explanation gave me a lot of information about what his level of concentration would be for the rest of the meeting. It also allowed the manager to share with the group what was on his mind.

. . . .

This example might be extreme, but there are other ways in which team members can be 'called out of the room' during an online meeting: by notifications on their computer or phone, or unexpected movement they catch out of the corner of their eye. In an office, Louise, who is attending the meeting from her desk, might be distracted by a group of people at the far end of the office, gathered round a screen and laughing; or Fred's flatmate might return home unexpectedly early and start making a lot of noise outside his home office.

These bits of information might not seem important enough to interrupt a conversation, but they could affect the dynamics of the discussion. It's worth creating the space for them to be communicated during a quick check-in round.

· ·

It had been a difficult meeting. As a virtual team, we were experiencing a breakdown in communication between the different task forces. At the same time, we all still respected each other and cared deeply about the project.

The team leader, looking flustered, thanked everyone politely and wrapped up the discussion. Just as she was about to close the meeting, Lorena, the designer, jumped in.

Everyone's eyes widened. There were vocalisations of surprise, of admiration.

And we all waved goodbye to each other with a smile.

· ·

MAKE YOUR MEETINGS MATTER

- Disagreements can lead to creative insights. Consider using some of the strategies in this chapter to keep the meeting on track.
- If no one disagrees in your team, you might want to review whether there is enough psychological safety.

28

Ending the meeting

Meetings usually end because people need to leave, there is nothing left to discuss or the tech is causing so many problems that we can't hold a proper conversation. In all three cases it's a good idea to end the meeting formally before everyone logs out, so that no one leaves feeling as if there is unfinished business. As humans, we tend to operate in cycles: we look forward to the end of the week so that we can start the next one with energy; we make new year's resolutions. Our lives are made up of beginnings and endings.

If you can see that you are running out of time, stop the meeting early. Ask if everyone can stay ten more minutes. If they can't, spend the last 5 minutes planning how you will continue the conversation: the follow-up discussion might only need to involve two or three of you; or perhaps you have enough momentum now to finish the conversation over the next two days on your collaboration platform.

If you run out of things to talk about, great! Celebrate your efficiency, close the meeting and do something else. There is nothing shameful about finishing a meeting early. Finally, if tech problems are making it difficult to talk to each other, move on to the chat or your collaboration platform to decide how to proceed.

WRAPPING UP THE DISCUSSION

One factor which has contributed to meetings gaining a bad reputation is that conversations can go on endlessly without reaching a useful conclusion. In the online world, it's easy to tune out of these conversations and start checking email, browsing the internet or doing some other online activity.

Furthermore, teams have a tendency to pay more attention to trivial issues than important, strategic ones – a phenomenon known as the 'bike-shed effect'. In his book *Parkinson's Law: Or the Pursuit of Progress*, C. Northcote Parkinson tells the story of a finance committee that approved an investment of £10 million in a nuclear power plant in 2½ minutes.[75] "That's efficient," I hear you say. But that same team later spent 45 minutes deciding what colour to paint the bike shed with, a project costing about £350.[76]

While difficult decisions are frequently left to the experts, people are happy to contribute to simpler discussions where the stakes are low. Look out for these discussions, as they can drain a team's energy and time. Conversely, trivial discussions help team members connect with each other, turning a work issue into a social one. In the online space, it's worth looking out for those moments when we can connect socially with each other.

ESCAPING A DOWNWARD SPIRAL

Getting stuck on an issue that really matters is a different story. As everyone starts wondering when the torture will end, it is worth saying out loud that the conversation is stuck in a loop. What you do in these situations is something you could include in your meeting charter (which is a good way of acknowledging that this will happen at some point – no team is perfect). You can use one of the following procedures, depending on the meeting and the type of conversation:[77]

- The fastest option is for you, or the person leading the meeting, to decide whether to end the discussion or keep it going. If the meeting is focused on helping one or two individuals, ask them whether the discussion is helping them. If it isn't, end it.

---

75   C. Northcote Parkinson, cited in Scott Keller and Mary Meaney (2017) 'High-performing teams: A timeless leadership topic', *McKinsey Quarterly*, June. Available at: www.mckinsey. com/business-functions/organization/our-insights/high-performing-teams-a-timeless-leadership-topic?cid=other-eml-ttn-mkq-mck-oth-1801

76   It gets worse: they also spent an hour discussing what new kind of coffee machine they should get, but decided to postpone the decision because they could not agree on how to spend the £20 budget for this new acquisition (see Keller and Meaney).

77   Sam Kaner (2014) *Facilitator's Guide to Participatory Decision-making*, John Wiley & Sons.

- Pick one element of the discussion, and focus on that.
- Set a time limit, then stop the discussion.
- Give everyone the chance to intervene one more time, then wrap up. If a decision needs to be made, agree on how this will be done, and by whom: for example, through a sub-team or an individual, asynchronously or another real-time discussion. (Remember that meetings should not be the only place where you make decisions in your remote team.)

If you need to continue the discussion asynchronously:

- Will you need to communicate in long form, expressing your ideas in full and having others comment on them? (For example, on a blogging platform or a shared document.)
- Do you need to gather more information (for example, data, articles) to help you make a more informed decision? Sometimes we go round in circles because we are missing information.

HAS EVERYTHING BEEN SAID?

"So, if no one has anything else to add, let's close this meeting and get back to work!"

That is quite an uninviting statement at the end of any kind of meeting (meetings *are* work), but in the online world, it's even worse. There might be somebody who has something to add, but they are finding it difficult to speak up as everyone else is already saying "Bye!" at the screen and waving their hands around. There is no opportunity to say, "Actually, there is something I wanted to say" as people get ready to go. Leaving an online meeting takes about 2 seconds, compared to the longer time it takes in a colocated space to gather your things, get up from your chair and walk out of a meeting room.

If some team members take a while to share their thoughts, or if the conversation has mainly involved a few people in the team, consider wrapping up the discussion in one of the following ways.

- Before closing the meeting, ask whether anyone has anything to add. Then hold the silence – by which I mean, let the silence continue beyond an uncomfortable length. Then, summarise what you have achieved in the meeting, or suggest an article to read, or remind team members of an upcoming event or milestone. Then ask again whether anyone has anything to add. It could be the case that during the time you have shared some extra information, somebody's cogwheels have been turning and now they are ready to speak.
- For teams not used to meeting online, end the session by asking everyone if there is anything they are still unclear about, or if they would like to add something. Include this in your agenda or meeting plan, and call it something inviting, such as: 'Final Thoughts' or 'Unspoken Words', rather than 'Any Other Business'.
- In larger teams, make sure that everyone knows where in the collaboration space they can continue the conversation. Some team members might have something to add, but they think they will need longer than 5 minutes, and so decide not to speak up. A reminder that conversations don't stop at meetings might be the only prompt that somebody needs to express their thoughts.

Hang around online afterwards

It's not unusual for team members to leave things unsaid at a meeting. Perhaps they have something to add that they don't want to share with the whole group, or they disagree with you, the manager, but didn't want to start an argument in front of the whole team.

It can feel isolating to come out of a team meeting without having found closure. Having seen everyone logging off, those working from home might let their thoughts simmer without sharing them with anyone else. However, if they see that someone is still around, they might message them: "Have you got five more minutes for a quick chat?"

That extra conversation with an individual can make a big difference to how we feel about the meeting as a whole. For that reason, if you know that a meeting will be difficult, make sure to schedule time afterwards to hang around visibly online, just in case someone wants to speak to you. Once you are sure that no one wants to do this, shut down your computer and take a well-deserved break.

. . . .

Cynthia, a project manager in a global organisation, was leading a challenging project involving employees from several countries. She had got to know her virtual team members very well, and knew that one of them rarely disagreed with the group so as not to disturb the status quo.

For that reason, Cynthia would pick up the phone after every meeting and ask that team member whether there was anything else he needed to say or clarify. There always was.

. . . .

MAKE YOUR MEETINGS MATTER

- Think about how your meetings end.
- Try to vary how you end your gatherings and, if necessary, plan the ending in advance.

29

The meeting wrap-up

Review the kind of meetings you hold in your team, and who is expected to attend. Is everyone clear as to why they are attending?

How do you decide which team decisions need to be made at a meeting? Can certain types of decisions be made using your collaboration ecosystem? Look for the best ways for team members to make decisions together.

Collectively or individually, check that everyone feels comfortable using the basic functions of your meeting platform.

How do you decide the content of your meetings? Can everyone contribute to it? Does your ecosystem allow you to easily co-create an agenda or plan? If not, what technology or processes do you need to introduce?

Would recording some of your meetings be useful to your team? How can you ensure that everyone feels safe during them?

Do you have different ways of starting a meeting? Do team members enjoy carrying out a ritual at the beginning of a team meeting? What questions or conversation prompts can you use to encourage everyone to speak to the group at the beginning of the meeting?

Do you share documents at your meetings? If not, would doing so make them more effective? If you share your screen, are you aware of whether it impacts the conversation?

What is the rhythm of your conversations like? Is there any room for silence, reflection or deep individual thinking?

In what ways do you tackle disagreement in your meetings? Would you benefit on some occasions from breaking out into groups during the meeting, to better understand each other's viewpoints?

How we leave a meeting tends to have a stronger impact on us if we are away from our team members than if we are working next to them. When planning meetings, think about how you will end them. Better still, design with your team a couple of ways to end your meetings, and rotate the responsibility for wrapping them up.

For longer meetings, what kind of questions can you ask half way through, to take the temperature in the team and change course of action, if needed?

Have you got a way of capturing what happens at the meetings, that is easily accessible within your workflow?

This part of the book ends with more detail on running two types of meetings:

- The workflow meeting – regular team meetings, similar to 'status meetings', which some of you might want to run to stay connected as a team and see each other regularly, even if you already have a system of visible teamwork.
- The hybrid meeting – meetings where some people are in the room together and others are online need to be run differently to those where everyone is behind their computers.

30

The workflow meeting

Meeting regularly to catch up on progress and coordinate next steps can be extremely valuable. However, these types of meetings can turn into cold reporting sessions that interrupt our work.

'Status meetings', with the sole aim of reporting on task-driven progress, can be replaced by online systems of 'visible workflow', updated by team members as the work gets done. Workflow meetings can then be used to ask for help or answer questions about our work: they remind us that we all affect each other's work – it's the flow of communication that is important here, not the status of what we are doing.

If your team members' schedules or geographic locations mean that it's difficult to meet regularly online, divide yourselves into sub-teams, or create a viable meeting schedule in smaller groups.

· ·

INSPIRATION

Members of the Happiness Team at Buffer are spread all over the world. They meet daily, twice a day, for about 10 minutes, scheduling their meetings to suit different time zones.

The teams in Europe and east coast of the USA meet at a time that suits both; later on, the latter group will meet with the west coast of the USA; while the next meeting takes place between the west coast and Asia, and so on. Even if there is nothing to discuss, these meetings create touchpoints for team members, helping them develop their communication rhythm.[78]

---

78   Carolyn Kopprasch (2020) 'One daily team meeting, across 5 time zones: Buffer's May happiness report', Buffer. Available at: https://open.buffer.com/buffer-may-happiness-report/

Through talking about their work with others, team members might realise that they are unaware of what's going on outside the team, such as initiatives in the organisation unconnected to your team's work. As a manager, you might be the person with up-to-date information that helps to clarify the team's activities within a wider context. Use your regular meetings to remind the team about the context in which they are operating, and how their work fits in with the wider organisation.

· ·

Maybe you feel that personally you have little to gain from these meetings: your work as a manager might be self-contained, and you regularly catch up with team members individually. If all that happens in these meetings is that you reconnect with your team members as a team – well, that is valuable in itself. Design your daily schedule in such a way as to allow you to take a break from deep work by attending these meetings, and focus on the value that you provide to team members, instead of the value that the meeting has for you.

SHOULD WE REPLACE MEETINGS WITH ASYNCHRONOUS, TEXT-RICH COMMUNICATION?

When you see team members every day, there is no need to come together in a meeting to go through work progress; it's preferable to use meetings for more strategic conversations. However, in the online space, it's a different story. Remember: people connect with each other in different ways. While some of you might need those virtual coffees, where you talk about anything except work to feel connected; others might prefer to connect through the work.

Workflow meetings can serve as a reminder of how we are connected to other team members, and in some cases, how our work is interconnected. Talking regularly about work with other team members connects individuals, and helps them feel valued – acting as a reminder that they are part of something larger than themselves.

On a personal note, as a curious person working online, I miss overhearing conversations or looking over people's shoulders when they are at their computers.

Workflow meetings can be a way of satisfying those team members who are curious by nature, who want to understand what others are working on, even when it doesn't impact their own work. Meetings can provide a space to have richer conversations about the work than those in a collaboration platform or project management tool.

CREATE A MEETING STRUCTURE

By having a set structure for your workflow meetings, you can save energy when running the meeting itself. Team members will know what to expect from the meeting and what their contribution needs to be. To some this might sound boring; but when the team is busy or going through change, a familiar structure can feel comfortable.

Depending on the work your team does, your workflow meetings can focus on the progress of tasks, or concentrate on the more general aspects of your work, both as individuals and as a team.

General catch-ups

Unless we are trying to overcome a specific obstacle or need help with a task, it can be difficult to know how to contribute to regular meetings as a team member. (And if we are busy or if we don't feel at our best during the meeting, it can take too much energy to know how to contribute.)

Consider having a set of questions to hand for those moments when you are uninspired. They can be focused on the individual and their work. For example:

- What are the most important decisions you need to make in the near future?
- What obstacles can you foresee?
- What discussions are you likely to have with people outside the team?

· ·

INSPIRATION

At freistil IT, team members use the DIRECT framework to help
them contribute information useful to themselves or others:

- Decisions they have taken lately
- Insight they have had recently
- Results they are proud of
- Emotions they have felt recently (for example, are they happy
  or sad about something)
- Contact they have made recently
- Trouble they are having

· ·

After coming across this framework in a blog post[79] by Jochen Lilich, the
company's founder, I added another area of conversation: giving Thanks
to someone in the team, making the framework: DIRECTT.

The components of DIRECTT are all the things we communicate to
our team members when they are near us. They are pieces of information
which are communicated frequently and spontaneously in the office. In
the online space, this framework unearths some of this information while
keeping meetings short.

(Remember to make space too for something that needs to be shared
but doesn't fit within the acronym.)

Having a structure to help team members contribute to the meeting
that includes reference to 'troubles' in the work, can surface problems
earlier on. It is also a strong signal that it's OK to ask for help, and creates
the conditions for psychological safety.

Task-based catch-ups

My favourite way to make the progress of work visible are Kanban boards,
and as I mentioned in Chapter 22, they can also guide you through a
meeting.

---

79   freistil IT (2017) 'Working out loud doesn't mean being noisy', 23 December. Available at:
      www.freistil.it/working-out-loud/

Online boards are great for visualising a team's workflow. If you are already using this kind of tool in your team, it can guide you through the meeting and help the process feel organic.

. . . .

I first came across this way of running update meetings at Management 3.0. We used Trello to guide us through weekly meetings. Our board consisted of a series of 'lists': 'Doing', 'Next Up', 'Completed', 'Ideas', etc. Each list had specific tasks labelled with the avatar of the team member working on them.

At the beginning of meetings, we focused on the 'Doing' list. We looked down the list to see whether anyone had anything to say about what they were working on, or whether anyone had questions or suggestions about what someone else was doing. If there was no progress on the task or nothing to report or ask, we moved on.[80] There was no need to go through the status of each task, as it was already visible.

. . . .

Key to this type of meeting is having a way of capturing any decisions or changes that affect tasks. For example, at the meeting you might discover that a task you thought of as completed was missing a vital step. In that case, the task would be moved from 'Completed' to 'Doing', with a note explaining why the change has been made. In this way, those not present at the meeting can track changes to workflow.

Snippets

Another structure to take inspiration from are 'Snippets', used at Google's management meetings,[81] where managers write up their updates ahead of discussion. Before the meeting, each team member writes in a shared document three to five things they have done since the last meeting, and/ or what they plan to do over the next period. These updates are then used to trigger follow-up questions, offers of help and useful information.

---

80   Management 3.0 (nd) 'How Trello can help your team self-organise'. Available at: https:// management30.com/blog/how-trello-can-help-your-team-self-organise/

81   Kim Scott (2017a) *Radical Candor: How to Get What You Want by Saying What You Mean*, Macmillan (Kindle Edition), location 3860.

You can adapt this easily to the online space. Make sure you agree a deadline by which updates should be posted, to give everyone enough time to review the document before the meeting. Don't set the deadline too far off from the meeting date, or some updates will become irrelevant by the time you meet.

THE INVISIBLE BENEFITS OF REGULAR MEETINGS

As well as providing an opportunity for you all to reconnect through the work, the workflow meeting is a good place for team members to exercise their facilitating skills. If you have a structure for your meetings, it's easier to keep the discussion on track, and rotating facilitators from one meeting to the other can be done quite painlessly.

Plus each facilitator brings a different energy to each meeting, which keeps everyone on their toes. Granted, some people do run meetings better (or faster, or with more charm, depending on what 'better' means to you), but the learning experience of being in charge of starting a meeting on time, keeping it on track and ending on time increases appreciation for well-run meetings, which leads to better participation in future meetings.

Moreover, regular meetings assist in identifying problems or obstacles early on. It might be easier for someone to mention casually that they are struggling with the work during a workflow meeting (as part of the first 'T' in the DIRECTT framework), than it is for them to write their troubles in a collaboration platform.

Don't break the habit of meeting regularly online. Once you stop, it's harder to start again.

31

Hybrid meetings

Hybrid teams – teams where some people work together in an office, while others work from elsewhere – present more challenges than those where all team members are dispersed. While the wide range of difficulties of leading a hybrid team are beyond the scope of this book, this chapter, in addition to everything we have covered so far, will make your life easier.

Even if you are running a fully remote team, this chapter will come in useful if you ever organise occasional, in-person meetings that some people can't get to, your team collaborates with a colocated team, or needs to dial into a client's office.

. . . .

AN UNEVEN PLAYING FIELD

"The guys in head office are having a meeting with someone who is going to show them the apps we will be using. Would you like to attend?"

Of course, I said yes. I was involved in the early stages of a pilot to develop new ways of collaborating online in a global organisation. A meeting had been arranged in the Swedish head-quarters with a consultant, and the project manager was attending remotely. Thinking I would benefit from attending, albeit online, she invited me along. It would be the first time I met those at the meeting.

Because of previous commitments, I joined the meeting half an hour late. The project manager interrupted the conversation to let everyone know that I had arrived, and asked everyone to switch from speaking Swedish to English, the official language in the company.

I blushed, but that was OK because I didn't have my camera on. I decided to keep it that way as I couldn't see anyone else online, just a set of slides. At the bottom-right corner I saw the profile picture of the meeting host, a friendly man with a round face and glasses. After 10 minutes, the speaker wrapped up the presentation, stopped sharing their slides, and then I saw nothing.

I already knew that the norm in this company was to hold audio-only meetings, but I had been expecting at least a webcam pointing to the corner of the room. To help me put names to voices, I sent a message to the project manager in the chat.

"Who's that lady speaking now?"

"Which lady?", the project manager replied.

"The one that just spoke."

"I'm not sure who you mean?"

"The one speaking *now*."

"That's not a lady, that's Frank!"

. . . .

Having read this book, you are probably thinking, '*Pilar, why on earth didn't you say something there and then? Or why didn't you ask them in advance to set up a webcam?*'

Well, I already felt like the group was accommodating me in more than one way: I hadn't been invited in the first place, and they had already switched languages halfway through. Although nowadays, after a few more years of working with clients, I would deal with this situation differently, what happened was an example of how remote employees find it difficult to ask for changes to how a meeting is run.

Sometimes, being the remote employee can feel like an imposition: it's difficult to ask most team members to change their behaviour to accommodate you. Although remote employees have a responsibility to make the meeting work for them, the more that you as team leader can level the playing field, the better the meeting will be for the team. Here are some things to consider.

ONE PERSON, ONE DEVICE

When possible, use the 'one person, one device' rule (or as Lisette Sutherland says, "when one person is remote, the whole team is remote").[82] This could mean that everyone sharing an office uses their own workstation, laptop or mobile at their desk or in a booth, rather than getting together in a meeting room.

Or those in the meeting room can log into the meeting with their individual devices. This levels the playing field, and those people not based in the office stop feeling like they are 'remote'. It also means that everyone has their own device and direct access to documents, can control their sound, camera, etc.

But let's face it: if you are in an office where you spend most of your time in front of a computer, to have a meeting with colleagues in a room together provides a welcome change. And talking to someone in the same building through a device, when you could look effortlessly and directly into their eyes, seems forced and unnatural. While this means that it might seem more natural to those colocated to hold the meeting as a hybrid, it does mean you are putting the needs of colocated team members first. If you do hold these types of meetings regularly, consider combining both approaches.

When you have only one device

If you decide (or need) to hold the meeting in one room and you only have one camera and one microphone available, colocated team members need to adopt behaviours that might feel unnatural. If you are using video, make sure that you can be seen by those at the other end of the camera. This might mean sitting at an awkward angle, or adjusting your position when speaking.

In addition, you can use more than one device to log in, and point different cameras to different parts of the room. You also need to signal that you are going to speak before doing so. On video, this might mean raising your hand, so that the person watching you through their screen knows where to direct their attention next; in an audio-only setting, mention your name every time you speak.

---

82   Lisette Sutherland (2015) 'When one person is remote, the whole team is remote', Collaboration Superpowers, podcast, 21 December. Available at: www.collaborationsuperpowers.com/69-when-one-person-is-remote-the-whole-team-is-remote/

BUDDY UP

Regardless of how well you know the person or people beaming in or calling into the office, they might be grateful to have a colocated 'buddy'. This person can double-check that the meeting remains 'remote friendly', and that anything that happens in the colocated space is communicated to everyone in the meeting. For example, if someone is shaking their head vigorously out of vision for the 'remotee', the buddy can let them know through chat or speech.

SLOW DOWN

When people are in the same meeting environment, the conversation picks up a rhythm: they notice signals that others want to speak, or that we haven't finished yet. When people are operating in two different environments (online and in the room), this can become tricky. The people in the room pick up on behaviours that remote team members can't even see.

As mentioned previously, slow down. When you pick up the conversation, double-check that remote team members haven't been waiting for a while to interject. When they are speaking and it looks like they are done, check that they were not just pausing for breath before you pick up the conversation.

Remember: while those in the room are using their ears for 360-degree hearing, remote participants are most likely wearing a headset, and will be more sensitive to sound. Leaving the door to the meeting room open to let in fresh air might seem like a good idea for those in the office, but it might let in unwanted noise from the corridor and other areas. Double-check with your remote members whether any changes in the physical location of your room are affecting them negatively.

DON'T OVER-HUDDLE

If you have a basic set-up (by which I mean a laptop with a webcam), those of you in the meeting room might be tempted to 'video huddle' in front of the camera, so that your remote team members can see all of you at the same time. If there are more than three of you in front of the webcam, it will get uncomfortable, both for those in front of the screen and those online.

Instead, agree with remote team members whether they prefer you to move the camera towards the person speaking, or if they are OK with hearing people whose faces they can't see.

MAKE SURE EVERYONE IS HEARD

Ensure that remote participants can hear everyone in the room, and that everyone in the room can hear all the remote participants. Use the checking-in time at the beginning of the meeting to practise speaking directly at the microphone, raising your voice slightly, or speaking more slowly, so that you can be heard and understood at the other end of the line. (For more on this, see Chapter 7.)

If some of you in the room are far from the microphone, you will need to project your voice. Speak directly to the microphone, or imagine that you are speaking to someone on the other side of the wall.

Remote first

If two people try to speak at the same time, and one is colocated while the other is remote, let the remote person speak first. It will be easier for the person sharing a space with others to find another suitable time to contribute.

TAKING NOTES

If you are used to capturing ideas on flip charts or whiteboards, what could you use instead? Are there any online alternatives you could use, or will you use your colocated aids and assign one person to capture your remote team members' ideas for them?

If you and your team members are used to attending meetings with laptops and capturing notes with them, be aware that keyboard noise might sound loud for those taking part online.

If your meetings are regular, consider changing how you share information. Sometimes you might want to run a session using only online tools, while in others you might prefer to encourage a more physical approach, integrating remote team members by buddying them up with colocated colleagues.

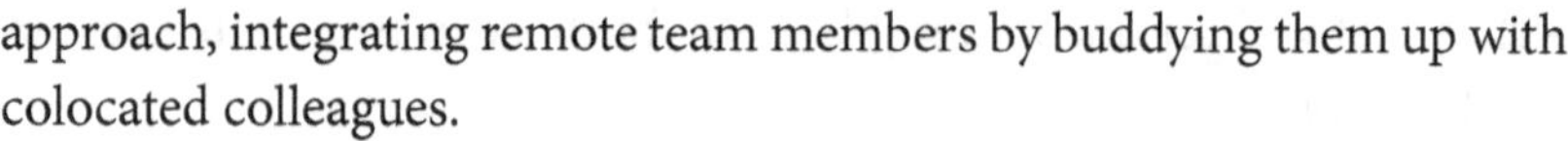

INSPIRATION

Clare Stankwitz, an agile coach I met in the community Virtual Team Talk, shared with me how she runs her hybrid meetings:

> We have 1 full-time remote team member, and 12 in-person folks, so it's a balancing act. I try to alternate whether I run the retro 100% using electronic tools v. buddying up the remote person with others and doing something more physical/in-person.[83]

FOLLOW UP WITH HIGH-QUALITY CONVERSATION

If you regularly run hybrid meetings in your team, set some time aside to meet with your remote team members on a one-to-one basis regularly, to check that they are happy with their involvement in them. For some team members it is difficult enough to speak up in any kind of meeting, and being in the minority ('beaming in') can make this harder. Once a person realises that they can get away with not saying much, they might start wondering whether their attendance is valued at all.

If a hybrid meeting has involved someone from outside your team, follow up with a written message or a quick conversation to make sure that there is nothing else they want to add or anything on which they have missed out. Make sure that whatever tool you are using to continue communication with them is working. For example, up until now, they might have communicated with you via email; but after meeting everyone else in the team and being a part of the discussion, they might prefer to be added to your collaboration platform in a dedicated channel or group.

---

83   Personal communication (conversation) with Claire Stankwirz in online Virtual Team Talk community, 2017.

BE PREPARED

Hybrid meetings take more preparation than fully colocated or online ones. If you and your team members find a rhythm and set-up which allows remote team members to feel as if they are in the room with you, continue down that road. You will achieve everything you set out to do, and will feel closer together (physically and psychologically).

However, if those in the same room forget at any point that there are 'remotees' at the other end of the webcam and/or microphone, the meeting will leave your remote team members feeling even more detached. Before you hold a hybrid meeting with more than two people in a colocated space, ask yourself:

- How many of us really need to be at the meeting?
- How much information can we share prior to the meeting?
- How far can we get with the discussion online?

If you do decide that you still need to go ahead with a hybrid meeting, keep it short.

Finally, if hybrid teams are the norm in your organisation and meetings are important to you, you will need to invest in technology. Setting up a space where hybrid meetings can be run efficiently and creatively is more affordable now. Invest in good microphones for the room, and look for webcams or other devices that zoom into people as they speak.[84] Not only will the investment make your meetings matter more, but it will also help remote employees feel valued.

When we meet in a room, we don't realise the amount of connection that goes on subconsciously. We don't pay attention to the range of interactions, or when and how they take place. In the blog post 'Tragedies of the remote worker: "Looks like you're the only one on the call"',[85] Scott Hanselman outlines many of the pitfalls of hybrid meetings mentioned in this chapter. He highlights those behaviours that make him feel

---

84   This article is a good place to get some recommendations: J. Elise Keith and Lisette Sutherland (2019) 'Can your meeting kit cut it?', *InfoQ*, 3 September. Available at: www.infoq.com/articles/can-your-meeting-kit-cut-it/

85   Scott Hanselman (2015) 'Tragedies of the remote worker: "Looks like you're the only one on the call"', 16 March. Available at: www.hanselman.com/blog/TragediesOfTheRemoteWorkerLooksLikeYoureTheOnlyOneOnTheCall.aspx

unappreciated and dispensable, such as not turning on webcams, or speaking far away from the microphone or speakerphone. Finally, he ends the article with frustration at not being part of those conversations that often happen once a meeting has officially ended: 'The meeting is over and they are hanging up. You can see their hand dropping to hit "End Call" and then someone starts mentioning something *totally important* and… dial tone.'

PART 4

THE KIT

Introduction

We now come to the 'techie bit', where we focus on how we attend those meetings – the section you won't find in books that focus solely on colocated meetings. The previous sections of this book have focused on making meetings work for your team. This part is about yourself and your own relationship with the technology.

Chapter 40 outlines a list of features commonly available to consider for when you are in the process of choosing a new meeting platform, or reviewing what your current one has to offer. This part of the book has no reflections or questions to help you 'make your meetings matter', as the content is more straightforward than previous sections.

As the technology is bound to advance rapidly, and meeting platforms are likely to appear and disappear in the market, I have not included recommendations of any products in this chapter. Instead, head over to onlinemeetingsthatmatter.com for a list of recommended platforms.

First, though, let's give some thought to how you show up in your meetings. You, after all, are the most important bit of kit.

32

Finding your best self

Our focus on technology can lead us to forget that the online world is made up of human beings. When I began running a business to help transition organisations to remote working, the first question people would ask was: "What tools do you use?"[86]

I bet that you have had conversations where others have told you how much they love their favourite meeting platform, without mentioning their favourite behaviours[87] of those attending. Technology is sometimes so shiny that we forget it's there to serve us in helpful ways.

Let's begin by thinking about how to make yourself comfortable during meetings.

YOUR POSTURE

As knowledge workers used to exercising our brain at work, we often ignore the effect that our body can have on our psychology. Mind and body don't exist in isolation from each other – although given the strain we put on our bodies in the name of 'hard work', we operate as if they do.

While your posture need not be perfect during meetings, make sure you consciously choose how you attend them:

---

86   Looking back, it's a similar question to what I was asked when I used to run a theatre company in the 1990s: "Where's your office?", or "Where do you do your shows?". The first thing that people want to know is how you practically do your work, never mind how you work with others, and the principles behind strong working relationships.

87   Indeed, sometimes the tech is the only thing in the meeting that doesn't give us grief. One of my collaborators put it beautifully. When we connected one afternoon on Skype and I asked him what his day had been like so far, he answered, "All right – we were in a meeting and it was getting difficult." "What platform were you meeting on?" "Ah, the problem wasn't with the tech, it was with the people."

- You can sit at your desk, upright, in full professional mode.
- You can have the meeting from your sofa, because you need a break from your desk.
- You can stand because you feel you need energy, or because you have been sitting down all day and need to stretch your legs.

Just add any other variation you can think of. You can be present at your meetings in whatever way you want, as long as you are aware of what your posture is doing to your body, and the effect it might have on those interacting with you.

SELF-AWARENESS

Have you heard of method acting? To portray a character's emotion truthfully, actors turn to a time in their lives when they experienced that particular emotion. I have always thought this was madness: one of the joys of acting is that you can have experiences that you would not go through in your real life. Why would you want to bring your own memories into a work of fiction?

There is a faster (and psychologically safer) way of accessing emotions: altering your posture or changing how you use your body. In the knowledge-worker world, there are a range of studies that show the connection between what our bodies do, and how we think or feel. One study with undergraduates showed that slumping at the computer can result in feeling less confident about your abilities as a worker; another concluded that holding a pen between your nose and mouth (which engages the muscles involved in smiling) can make you feel happier; and finally, making a fist with your hand can increase self-esteem.[88] While these conclusions have been drawn from single experiments and will not work for every person, they remind us of the importance of self-awareness. Knowing what your body is doing is not only important when monitoring the signals it sends to others, but also in understanding how it can affect your own state of mind.[89]

---

88   Kelly McGonigal (2009) 'Change your posture', *Psychology Today*, 5 October. Available at: www.psychologytoday.com/gb/blog/the-science-willpower/200910/change-your-posture

89   I have not included here the 'power pose' made famous by Amy Cuddy through a TED

Self-awareness helps you avoid unnecessary tension in your body. Sitting in the same posture in front of a computer, while listening attentively to others, can cause tension in the neck, shoulders, lower back, thighs and jaw. If you are not aware of your muscles tensing up, this can result in a build-up of tension which might cause pain in the future.

Moreover, slumping in a chair can affect how we breathe. The centre of our breathing lies around our belly, with our diaphragm contracting and relaxing to change the air pressure in our lungs. A slumped posture can put pressure on that area, restricting its movement and affecting the quality of our breathing, however slightly.

YOUR BODY PRODUCES YOUR VOICE

How you sit or stand affects the energy and tone that your voice carries. This means that even if you are attending an audio-only meeting, you still need to monitor what your body is doing. Slumping can remove energy from your voice (as it affects your breathing), and you might be perceived as disinterested or uncaring rather than relaxed (Figure 10).

Although posture affects different people to varying degrees, it is worth being aware of how you are using your body (and that includes your face), even when you are not on video.

Figure 10: Movement during breathing

Talk. The results of the study, which showed that adopting the 'power pose' had an effect on the levels of testosterone produced, have not been replicated by anyone else. This even led one of the co-authors of the study to admit that the evidence against the effect of the power pose was too strong to be ignored. Amy Cuddy (2012) 'Your body language may shape who you are', TEDGlobal, video, June. Available at: www.ted.com/talks/amy_cuddy_your_body_language_may_shape_who_you_are

ADJUSTABLE DESKS

During video meetings, do you keep your head in the same position as you stare at the monitor? When this happens, your neck can get stiff, your shoulders tense up and your eyes become dry.

If you have been working at a computer for a while before you start a meeting, why not put a couple of books or a box under your monitor, to change the height of your eyeline? Adjusting your posture might prevent that extra bit of stiffness from creeping up; and if you can stand, you could consider working at an adjustable desk.

. . . .

I was really jealous of my friend Lisette's standing desk. Not only could she stand while she worked (which feels cool to me), but she could raise and lower her desk at the push of a button, which looked impressive on-screen.

Whenever she did this at the beginning of our meetings, I would always think (and frequently said), "I want one!" Finally, I did buy one, and now I find it strange to work at desks with a fixed height. (And I'm the one who makes others jealous, as I raise and lower my desk during meetings just by pressing a button!)

. . . .

Organisations which have implemented hot-desking or activity-based working[90] often have adjustable desks for their employees. An increasing number of homeworkers are purchasing them too; I have even seen a home-made version at the co-working space I regularly use.

Meetings are the perfect moment to use a standing desk. You are unlikely to be using your keyboard and mouse as much as during regular work, so you can be more physically free.

Standing might give you that extra bit of energy that helps you stay focused, and it makes you more mobile. Standing up can have a positive effect during meetings, although not the one you would expect. In a study

---

90   Activity-based workplaces have different types of areas around the building, designed to help carry out different activities. Instead of everyone having their own desk and sitting according to departments or teams, people are free to use different work areas, depending on the kind of work they need to do: quiet zones for high-concentration work, collaborative areas for working with others, or café-style zones for light work, such as email.

from 1999, the researchers looked at the effect that standing up or sitting down had on meetings. The experiment incorporated 111 groups of 5 people, 56 of whom were standing up, and 55 sitting down. The results showed that although sitting down in meetings did not produce better results than standing meetings,[91] they were 34% longer.

This piece of research does not really explore the reason for the difference in meeting duration resulting from sitting or standing – we can only speculate. Perhaps standing up made people more tired, and in an attempt to end the meeting sooner, they picked up the pace (or they stopped contributing to the discussion to get through the agenda as fast as possible!). Or maybe standing kept the energy up in the group, increasing the meeting pace.

In any case, in the context of modern knowledge work, where we spend so much time sitting down in front of a computer, meetings seem an ideal moment to change your posture, stretch your back and be a bit more mobile. On the flip side, there also have been articles warning of the dangers of standing desks, and articles challenging those studies. At the end of the day, you need to monitor what is best for you. My guess is, a little bit of both.

GO WIRELESS

If you prefer to stand during meetings, a wireless headset will give you more freedom of movement. This can even be quite fun if you turn up early to a meeting, and then go off to make yourself a cup of tea while everyone else is catching up on personal stuff. You can still be part of the conversation from your kitchen.

A wireless headset also allows you to grab anything from your desk (or from under it!) during the meeting, without jolting your head by being attached via a cable to your computer. Plus you are less likely to keep your head in the same position, and risk tensing up your shoulders and neck.

---

91   Allen C. Bluedorn, Daniel B. Turban and Mary Sue Love (1999) 'The effects of stand-up and sit-down meeting formats on meeting outcomes'. *Journal of Applied Psychology* 84(2): 277–285.

THE DANGERS OF WORKING FROM ANYWHERE

I have attended meetings (mainly community of interest meetings) where people were logging on from public transport: a busy train or bus. I have even felt a little bit seasick when someone decided to leave their office in the middle of a meeting, mobile in hand, unaware of how much their handheld camera was moving up and down and side-to-side as they took the stairs, crossed the road and got into their car.

While I enjoy all this to a point because it means that people are attending the meeting in spite of needing to be on the move, it can become uncomfortable for everyone else. And as time goes on, this stops being a novelty and becomes an annoyance.

....

I am still amazed by what technology allows us to do. I was born in 1972, so I have been lucky enough to experience the world before the internet and other technology exploded, and can appreciate everything it allows me to do that I couldn't before.

I used to read *The Jetsons* (a Hanna-Barbera comic – the equivalent of *The Flintstones*, but instead of the family living in the past, they lived in the future). People's faces popping up on video has ceased to be something I found funny in *that comic* and is now part of my everyday life.

....

If you decide to attend a meeting on the move, just pop a message in the chat box saying that you will be off-camera for five minutes. Turn your camera off, stick your phone in your pocket or your bag, and switch the video back on when you have settled down.

If you are sharing text on the screen, those attending from a smartphone will have difficulty reading it. Plus if you are all working on a shared document and you want to add something to it during the meeting, it's fiddly to do that from a phone.

If you are planning a project or event, analysing data or creating documents, it's more practical to be sitting in front of a computer where you can easily pull up documents and edit them, accelerating your workflow.

Furthermore, if we are sitting comfortably on our sofa with our laptop, or walking in the street, holding our mobile phone in front of us, we are likely to let the person leading the meeting (who will most likely be at their desk) take responsibility for making notes, sharing data, updating documents, etc.

Attending meetings from any kind of location could easily turn into the group norm: 'We are so comfortable with each other that we meet from anywhere.' A norm that develops from a good place can result in dependency on the leader to move meetings forward; at worst, it can lead to social loafing, where a casual attitude means that one or two people end up doing the annotating and detailed thinking, while everyone else just shows up, expecting to be led fully.

TAKE BREAKS

Attending an online meeting can be more tiring than being present at a colocated one. If your meeting is long, take a break. How long is 'long' will depend on the kind of meeting you are holding: if the content is light, you can probably go on for 90 minutes. But if you need to be concentrating for the whole session and you are looking through documents on your computer at the same time, you might want to step away from your screen after an hour.

During breaks, avoid doing anything that involves a screen. Try to rest your eyes, and move your body to combat stiffness. Resist the temptation to go over to your mobile or carry out any other activity at your computer. Instead, find a window you can look out of, or if you are in an office space, find a large space to look across.

If during the meeting you feel you have been staring at the screen for long but it's not the right moment to suggest a break, rest your eyes. Place a short message in the chat to alert people you are still with them and listening, and close your eyes. You might even want to switch your webcam off.

As mentioned previously, you can change the position of your neck by raising or lowering your adjustable desk by a couple of centimetres, moving your webcam longitudinally, or raising it by placing a book or other solid object under it.

Lastly, don't forget to have some water or other drink available – but remember that if you are wearing a headset with a microphone next to your throat, you might want to mute yourself as you drink. And if you need to snack during the meeting, don't forget to turn off your microphone. If your table manners are dodgy, turn your video off too!

33

Changing your
space and focus

Have you ever been tidying up your desk in your home office, realised that you had left your smartphone on the kitchen table, gone to the kitchen and forgotten what you were supposed to be doing there?

Walking through a door can indeed cause a small memory lapse. This could be because many years ago, entering a new environment could mean a potential danger zone filled with predators: it required our full attention. In the present day, as we walk through a door, our brain interprets this as a cue to focus on our new surroundings, at the expense of forgetting whatever was on our mind a few seconds before.[92]

In the colocated workspace, going into a meeting usually involves stepping into a different space or setting. We leave our other work behind, and concentrate on the meeting itself. However, when we attend online meetings, we do this from the same physical space where we do our other work: same desk, chair and computer. And because we don't need to walk down a corridor to the meeting, we leave it until the very last minute to pop in. As a result, we spend the first five minutes trying to be fully present and focused.

Taking a break away from your environment before attending your meeting, switches your focus. If you are working from home, stop your other work 10 minutes earlier and take a 'comfort break'. If you are in an office and can use a different room, do so; or a few minutes before the meeting, close down those applications you won't need at the meeting, take a break away from your desk and when you return, go straight into the meeting. If you are working from a co-working space, look for an area in a different part of the venue. (If you are about to join a new co-working space, find one that has meeting booths or chairs.)

---

92   Dr Karl (2012) 'Can walking through a doorway make you forget?', *ABC Science*, 21 February. Available at: www.abc.net.au/science/articles/2012/02/21/3436001.htm

. . . .

My friend Judy and I laughed (and blushed) on the first day of our workshops on facilitating online learning, as we confessed to participants that we brushed our teeth and put on perfume when attending online meetings. If you have difficulty tuning into these meetings right from the start, find a little personal ritual to help you focus as soon as you enter the meeting space.

. . . .

TOOLS AND MULTIPLE WINDOWS

Just as you would gather your notebook and papers for a colocated meeting, make sure you have everything you need when you turn up online:

- Have you got somewhere to take notes?
- Are all the documents that team members will be using during the meeting open and ready?
- If your meeting agenda or points of conversation are out in an online tool or document, is that handy?
- Can you see all the windows you will need during the meeting?

. . . .

When I run idea-generation meetings, I feel like a DJ: I need the meeting platform to be visible so that I can see people's faces. If I have to share my screen, that requires some tweaking; meanwhile, there can be a document or app for the group to gather notes, which requires another window.

Finally, I always have a stack of paper sticky notes where I can quickly jot down any thoughts that come up during the meeting. They take up less space on my desk than a notebook.

I also have a glass of water handy. I make sure it's not a tall glass which can be knocked over easily as I wave my hands around in animated conversation.

. . . .

Although my own rituals might not affect my efficiency during the meeting, the ritual itself ensures that I am fully present as soon as it starts.

Figure out what you need to be fully present. Make a note of what helps you be at your best, and make the time to be totally ready before you meet your team.

34

Small habits amplified

I was wrapping up a follow-up session with a workshop attendee. I could see that she was digesting the advice I had given her and had become nervous. She was biting her nails.

The camera magnifies our habits and mannerisms. There is little distance between the person on the screen and the observer, we have little 'air' to dampen our little habits. I am particularly sensitive to signs of nervousness like nail biting, but in the colocated space I can shift my focus away by concentrating on someone's eyes. In the online space, that is extremely difficult to do.

Once you get used to meeting online and are comfortable in front of the camera, you will become less self-conscious. That is a good place to be: staying focused on the conversation and other people, instead of thinking of how we are coming across; but this doesn't mean that we should stop being self-aware.

Little habits can impede clear communication. For example, a member of a team I worked with kept putting a pen in front of her mouth when she was speaking. As her speech was laid back and the quality of her microphone only just acceptable, waving a pen in front of her lips made it difficult to understand her.

These habits are so small and harmless on their own that I only point them out if they are really damaging the conversation. They are part of people's identity, and tend to arise when they are anxious, or comfortable in the meeting and have let their guard down. For those reasons, I also rarely point them out. But I am bringing them up here while I have your attention, to raise your own self-awareness.

- Do you have any small habits that might get in the way of communicating with others?

- Anything that might distract them from listening or talking to you?

While I don't recommend looking at your own stream during video meetings (more on this in Chapter 35), you might as well use them as mirrors now and then, to help you notice things of which you would otherwise be unaware. Regularly attending video meetings might just be the experience you need to notice those habits that can get in the way of forming a strong connection with others.

<u>35</u>

Showing your best self

The other day, my neighbour Jennifer knocked on my door just as I was finishing my dinner. I was eating salmon in a spinach and peppercorn sauce, so before I opened the door I gave my teeth a quick brush. I didn't want to greet her with a smile featuring the remnants of my meal!

Whereas I love team meetings being informal, I believe we have a responsibility to do as much as we can to avoid making others feeling uncomfortable. As well as brushing your teeth before video meetings (not *during* them – believe me, I have seen it done!), here are some other things you might want to consider.

WEBCAM POSITION

Before you enter a meeting, check your webcam position. Check that the lens is not pointing straight up your nose, for example (Figure 11), and that others can see your face clearly. If you can, have the whole upper half of your body visible, so that when you use your hands, they come into view. (This can be difficult to do, but it's worth a try.)

Figure 11: Check your webcam position

If you are using two monitors, place your webcam and everyone else's video stream on the same monitor. In this way, when you look at everyone else you will end up facing the camera. There might be times when you are sharing a screen on your second monitor, and your attention needs to be on your work rather than on your team members – don't worry about that. Breaking that intense feeling of being watched, due to everyone looking in the same direction all the time, can be a good thing. But in general terms, facing the camera helps you to maintain a sense of conversation and connection.

Although you don't need to become obsessive about your set-up (you are having a meeting, not shooting a film), be aware of how your face is lit. While unflattering lighting is not a big problem, having a window behind you can place your face in darkness and prevent those in the meeting from reading your face.

LOOKING INTO THE CAMERA

One of the things we miss when talking to others online is eye contact. One quick way of faking this is looking at the camera, so that the other person feels like you are looking directly at them.

While I know that some people find this easy to do, and it does help me feel like they are making eye contact, I haven't been able to adopt this practice myself.

Looking into the camera means that I'm not looking at the face of the person I'm talking to. Whereas in the colocated space I tend to look at people's eyes (the face is too big for it to be wholly in focus), online – and especially when people's video boxes are not that big – I'm able to take in the whole face.

We know that the experience of talking to others over video is different to sharing the same physical space. Hopefully you and your team members can find a different way of connecting that doesn't involve a simulation of eye contact. You can find out what works for you only through experimentation.

. . . .

MIRROR, MIRROR, ON THE WALL...

Being able to see myself on my screen feels similar to talking to someone in a café, when there is a mirror behind them. No matter how much I want to connect with the other person, my eyes are always drawn to the mirror, and I end up staring at my reflection. I have no idea what this says about me as a person, but I do know it doesn't help my interaction with others. When I look at myself, I focus on my appearance, when I should be focusing on what others are saying and doing instead.

As a result, during meetings I often switch off my own video stream, especially when I'm talking to someone I know quite well. I want to focus on the other person, and that tiny square with my image gets in the way. Seeing myself also switches on my 'performance gene', and I end up thinking more about how I'm coming across than about what I'm trying to communicate.

. . . .

Of course, there are advantages to seeing yourself on the screen beyond checking whether you have spinach between your teeth. You can:

- Monitor your facial expressions – for example, to check that you are not inadvertently showing confusion
- Check that your appearance isn't distracting others – for example, when your hair suddenly starts covering your face
- Adjust your camera or turn on the feature that blurs your background, if unexpected distractions start happening behind you

However, once you have checked that your lighting is OK and that your background is not distracting everyone else, consider switching off your own video stream, and turning your full attention to the other person.

During a small study on the effects that seeing your own video stream can have on team meetings, researchers at Marquette University, USA discovered that students able to see their own faces were at a disadvantage compared with those who couldn't. The experiment involved two groups of people who had to solve a problem through communication and collaboration during online meetings. In one group, individuals could see their own image, while in the second group, they couldn't.

The results of this one-off, lab-based experiment concluded that 'viewing oneself leads to a reduction in team performance and individual satisfaction'.[93] Moreover, individuals were more satisfied with communication throughout the meeting when they could not see themselves on the screen. As a result, the authors recommended that video communication systems include the ability to remove one's image from the screen. Some video meeting applications have that functionality already, but if your platform does not give you the option to stop seeing yourself, you can always place a sticky note on your image on the screen.

Not quite what I meant

---

93   Martin D. Hassell and John L. Cotton (2017) 'Some things are better left unseen: Toward more effective communication and team performance in video-mediated interactions'. *Computers in Human Behavior* 73(August): 200–208, p. 201. Available at: www.sciencedirect.com/science/article/pii/S0747563217301966. Dan Misener (2017) 'How a sticky note could make you more productive at work', *CBC News*, 4 April. Available at: http://www.cbc.ca/beta/news/technology/videoconferencing-workplace-productivity-1.4053566

Although one study does not a hard-and-fast rule make, it is worth thinking about how seeing ourselves on the screen can affect the way in which we engage with others. Furthermore, one of the reasons why people resist switching on their webcam during meetings is because they don't like seeing themselves on-screen. Using a tool that enables you to 'hide yourself' (even if that tool is a sticky note), can give video meetings a chance.

36

Behind you!

Just as you can be in control of whether or not you see yourself on-screen, you can choose how much others see of your physical space. If you are working from home, you can decide whether others can see your laundry or someone preparing food in the background. Depending on how casual you and your team members are with each other, opening the doors to your home life might not be a concern. However, if you are meeting people outside your team, giving them access to your personal life in this way might not be appropriate.

Our background is part of our set-up: we need to pay attention to it, and look at the ways that we would prefer it not to affect our meetings. If you have a distracting background (if you are in a busy office or co-working space) or if you prefer not to invite team members into your home, make some changes to your surroundings.

If you don't have a dedicated office space at home, a screen divider can separate your workspace from the rest of the room.

. . . .

I often work from my flat, in a little corner in the lounge. In my previous set-up, the webcam on my laptop showed a wall behind me, with colourful sticky notes and a cartoon-infested calendar. I was happy for people to see that. I don't mind people seeing that I like cute cartoons and that I use sticky notes – it adds informality to professional interaction, which reflects my preferred mode of collaboration.

Now that I have a standing desk, I prefer to attend meetings from there. However, my webcam points to that part of the lounge that I prefer people not to see. It can be messy, which is no longer cute. It's also the area where we lay out the laundry, so now I place a room divider there during meetings: instead of making sure my background is clear, I pull out the screen and place it behind me. Plus, if my husband is at home, he can happily walk around without feeling like he is disturbing me, or distracting those on the other end of the webcam.

In a way, a screen can physically and psychologically prevent work/non-work life interference.

. . . .

If you are attending meetings from a busy office, there might not be much you can do to change your background. If you are stuck at your desk, where there is a lot of 'people traffic', point your webcam at an area where there is not much movement. (As mentioned previously, if your background becomes distracting, consider switching off your webcam for a while.)

When you use a meeting room, try to sit with your back to a wall rather than a glass partition – unless you want those in the meeting to feel like part of your office environment, in which case, make sure they can see your office. As you can see, how you operate depends on what you want to achieve. There is no best practice around this.

BLURRING YOUR BACKGROUND

Some applications have a feature that allows your background to be blurred. This means that you can get rid of any distractions behind you, without having to worry about finding a quiet space. It also allows you to hold your meetings at home without worrying about the state of your room, or putting up a screen.

I still haven't decided whether or not I like this feature. On the negative side, it tends to fire off the fan in laptops; and at the time of writing, the technology sometimes blurs the edges of a person too. On top of that, our background is a reminder of our context. I would say that sometimes this is part of our identity, so always consider whether it's better to blur your background or to tidy up the space behind you.

37

Mastering the tech

"Hang on, I'm not sure how to switch this webcam on… Let me see… Here, can you see me now?"
"No."
"And now…?"
"No, we still can't see you."
"Let me see, maybe if I restart this thing here…"
"Yes, now we can see you, but we can't hear you…"

And so it goes on. Ten minutes into the meeting, and we are still waiting for everyone to be ready to start.

In my parallel career as a voiceover artist, clients usually book me for one-hour sessions. I always turn up at least 10 minutes early so I have time to use the toilet, ask for some water and do whatever I need to do to be in front of the microphone and ready to go, right on the hour.

I do the same thing when I attend an online meeting. A few minutes before the meeting is due, I close whatever I'm working on, gather any documents I might need, get out my headset and test the tech. At the start time, I'm ready to go.

BUILDING YOUR COMPETENCE

There is no way around it. When working in a remote team, you need to master the technology and be comfortable using devices. You cannot let poor use of technology get in the way of effective communication.

Mastering technology is a skill. If you have started running online meetings recently, pay careful attention to how you use the platform. There will be a period during which it will take time for you to set up and during which you will need to check that both you and your applications are ready to go, before you start.

As you get used to meeting online, you will probably adjust your set-up. You might discover that you want to do other things during the meeting in addition to talking and listening, for example:

- Share links to documents or videos
- Share your screen so that others can see what you are working on
- Refer to your calendar often
- Insert tasks into your project management tool as the discussion progresses

If you decide to incorporate a range of online tools or applications into your meetings, consider using more than one device or screen.

. . . .

When I first started attending video meetings on the Zoom platform, I noticed that if I pulled up my project management tool, the meeting platform would disappear behind it.

Instead of adding a second monitor to my set-up, I used a tablet to view the project management tool. In that way, I could see everyone on the screen while interacting with the other tool.

(Using a second screen or device also has the benefit of making you move your head now and then, helping you to loosen your neck muscles.)

. . . .

MORE THAN ONE THING AT A TIME

As you become more familiar with your tech, you will feel more comfortable carrying out small tasks during the meeting, such as taking notes, adding notes to your calendar, updating task cards in your project management tool, etc.

This is regular meeting behaviour: it's unlikely for participants to do nothing but talk and listen. Online meetings usually involve taking notes, or looking for information in documents or online. However, carrying out different tasks while conversing can become distracting or counterproductive, so it's worth being aware of when you lose focus.

Some red flags to look out for:

- You realise that you haven't heard what has just been said.
- You ask questions that have been asked already, and answered!
- Team members tell you, "Yes, we've already discussed that."

It's also worth remembering that 'multitasking' during a meeting can make you come across as distracted. If you are regularly looking away from the screen or shifting your attention between devices, let your team members know what you are doing. This is one of those times when you have to communicate deliberately what others would pick up through visual cues in the colocated space.

USE THE MUTE BUTTON WISELY

Back in Part 2: Relationships, I suggested keeping your microphone open during meetings, unless you are somewhere particularly noisy or distracting to others. Keeping your microphone open means that it is easier to keep communication flowing, as communication is not just made up of sentences, but also of the odd 'Hmm', 'Er…' and spontaneous laughter.

However, keeping our microphone open can interfere with communication if we are making sounds of which we are not aware. Tapping your foot against your desk or clicking your pen can distract your teammates. If you are taking notes on your computer, know that the sound of your typing might go straight into someone's ears, which can be seriously distracting. Learning how to use your microphone, and how to mute it and unmute it quickly, is a skill worth mastering.

If you are using a headset, make sure your microphone is not too close to your nostrils and mouth, especially if you have a cold, as sounds from your nose will travel down the line. Similarly, if you are using the microphone on your laptop, be aware that your fan can kick into action and cause distracting background noise.

If you are in a quiet environment, using the inbuilt microphone for your computer and standing at an adjustable desk, avoid facing away from the microphone as you will become quiet to others.

These are all little things I have picked up during meeting a range of people online in varied circumstances – if you have been connecting with others online for a while, you will have noticed similar things too.

THE HEADPHONE–MICROPHONE COMBINATION

As mentioned previously, I attend most online meetings from the lounge in my flat, using only a cheap pair of headphones. I use the microphone on my laptop, which is pretty good, and even though it is not directly in front of me, it picks up my voice well. (If the fan kicks in, I switch onto a headset.)

This combination of headphones and computer microphone serves me well, but if I have the window open, or am attending a meeting from my co-working space, I use a set of microphone earbuds, so that background noise can be filtered out.

Now, I can hear you thinking, '*What about a wireless headset? You were recommending we use one just a few chapters ago...*' Well, I do use one every now and then, but ironically, because it's heavier than earbuds, I feel less comfortable.

It's a matter of experimenting until you find what works for you.

Some people prefer to dispense with headphones completely and listen through their computer's audio or external speakers. While listening through external speakers can cause problems (such as other people's voices echoing), I have seen plenty of people attend meetings using their laptop's speakers without it affecting the conversation. There are also portable audio conference devices, which can give you decent audio without headphones.

Personally, I like to hear people's voices directly in my ears – which, when you think about it, is not how we hear each other when we share the same physical space. But you might be different, so experiment with your audio until you find the set-up that suits you best.

38

Internet connection problems

The greatest barrier to having successful online meetings is neither people checking their email in the background, nor whether they are well facilitated, nor even an inability to come to a decision within a limited amount of time.

It's the stability of our internet connection. Do not underestimate that. Hopefully at some point, some of you will read this and say: "Broadband speeds? Unreliable WiFi? That's so 2020!" In that case, feel free to skip this section.

Meanwhile, if you still live in a world of variable internet speeds, you need to have a contingency plan for when meetings are disrupted by choppy connections. Especially if you are working in places that you have not worked from before (for example, a new café or on the road), you and your team will want to check your connections using an online broadband speed test (just search online for 'check internet speed').

Once you are in the meeting, if you are having connectivity issues, assess whether you are all having problems or if it just one person's connection that is giving you grief. In either case, you might want to begin by switching off your video (see Chapter 11). Be prepared for the tone and the rhythm of the meeting to change; and, as mentioned previously, make sure that if you don't have anyone acting as facilitator (or chair), that you agree on one before you switch to audio-only. Having a person leading the discussion can make up for the sudden loss of visual cues.

If you experience echo or audio delays, speak slower and in shorter sentences, so it's easier for the conversation to move backwards and forwards.

IT WAS ALL GOING SO WELL...

You might be about to wrap up a meeting when the broadband starts playing up. In that case, pause the conversation, acknowledge that there are technical problems, and that you will need to ask a speaker to repeat what they have said, if their speech becomes choppy or unintelligible. Everyone should be comfortable slowing down the conversation to make sure you can all still understand each other. Remind individuals that they can switch to the chat if the connection is breaking down at their end. Finally, slow down your own speech, and expect interruptions, as there will be delays.

Sometimes it is not your team members' internet connections that fail, but the platform you are using. It is worth having an alternative platform that you can all easily jump on to when tech gives you problems. If a new meeting needs to be set up, assign one person to do this, then hop off one-by-one. Make sure you have a backchannel ready (for example, a channel in your collaboration platform), in case there are problems with getting on to the second platform. If some of your team members are unsure about using the new technology, one of you can stay behind on the original platform to guide them through.

If you are transitioning to a remote set-up, ensuring that everyone has stable, high-speed internet should be high up on your list of priorities.

39

Choosing your
meeting platform

A book on online meetings would be incomplete without a good, chunky chapter on choosing an online platform. I have left this chapter for the end of the book to make sure you have already thought about what kind of meeting resources and experience you need and want. It can serve as a summary, as we have covered many of the meeting practices already mentioned.

I have favourite online platforms and those I try to stay away from, but this can vary from month to month as they keep evolving. Platforms I didn't enjoy using and thought would have disappeared by now have turned out to be stable, reliable meeting places with unique and useful features. Conversely, platforms I was fond of suddenly developed unhelpful customer service, and I began to wonder whether I should continue recommending them to clients and friends.

Of course, some of you will have little choice as to what meeting platform you can use in your organisation; so I prefer to stay 'platform-agnostic' for now and concentrate instead on their features. If you are stuck with the only tool available in your organisation, it is still worth reading through this list, as the platform might have those features already, but you are unaware of them, or they might be added by the developer at a later date. There is always the possibility that the tech you have access to will change as your company's IT develops, or when you move on to another job.

WHICH FEATURES, WHICH TOOLS?

Chris Slemp, the person behind Whichtoolwhen.com, recommends that teams don't get wrapped up in debates about features and tools, rather than get involved in discussions which drive better decisions around how to use those tools. What are our values as a team? What are the things we want to get out of collaboration? What values do we have as an organisation?[94]

For example, if your team values transparency, you might want a tool where it is easy to record and share the recordings of your meetings. Or, if you meet frequently with external clients and most of you work from home, you might want to blur your background at the click of a button.

There are practical considerations when choosing a tool or a platform for your meetings. In her list of tips for leading online meetings, Nancy Settle-Murphy reminds us that not everyone might have equal access to the tools. If the meeting platform requires high bandwidth, will this disadvantage those team members with a poor internet connection? If you need to download an application to have the meeting, might this be blocked by some company firewalls?

Finally, avoid overloading your meetings with tools. It's tempting to have different tools for taking notes, capturing actions or making decisions. As Settle-Murphy advises: 'First assess whether a particular meeting or technology is likely to enhance or accelerate your meeting results.'[95] If you are a heavy note-taking team, look for a platform with an integrated note-taking feature which can be easily accessed once the meeting is over.

Regardless of the meeting platform you adopt, learn how to use it properly. Find out which default settings can be changed to be able to run the meeting in the way that best suits your team, not in the way the platform developers imagined.

Finally, don't forget to train everyone! (Chapter 21 was some chapters ago, so I just thought I would remind you of the importance of doing so.)

Now, given that we are almost at the end of this book, I'm assuming that you have done enough thinking about how you want to run your meetings, and know what you would like to happen in them. What features are essential in a meeting platform and what are the 'nice to haves'? Make a list of these features, and start the search for the platform most likely to suit your team. Then, move on to the next chapter.

---

94   Virtual Not Distant (2017) 'WLP144: Designing a development programme for managers of remote teams', 26 October, podcast. Available at: www.virtualnotdistant.com/podcasts/training-remote-managers

95   Nancy Settle-Murphy (nd) '120 Essential Tips for Leading Amazingly Productive Virtual Teams', tips 23–24. Available at: www.guidedinsights.com/tips-guides

40

Desirable features in a meeting platform

Now that you have your own wish list, let's see if there is anything else we can add to it.

CHAT FUNCTION

An online platform without a chat function limits your interactions. In an online meeting, any little sound of agreement, small interaction or quick question easily feels like an interruption and can affect the flow of conversation. You can use the chat to add information not essential to the conversation. In addition, it can give everyone an idea of what is going on in team members' minds, and what the 'temperature' is in the meeting.

A chat function enables you to share website links, so that others can check them out in their own time and at their own pace. It's one of the benefits of meeting online. The chat is also the place where someone can say that they quickly need to reboot their computer, or that they have to go and get a glass of water and will be back in a second. It's an essential backchannel which can keep the team in sync without chopping up the conversation.

Depending on how your team likes to communicate, you might want to look for a platform that includes emoticons and stock phrases in the chat. However, be careful. An increasing number of communication tools and social media platforms are including stock phrases and preconstructed sentences to speed up communication. This means gradually risking losing our own voices in written communication in exchange for saving time. Beware of starting to use developers' phrases, rather than your own.

BREAKOUT ROOMS

This feature is a bit of a luxury, but it can take your meetings to another level if there are more than five or six of you in the team. However, a breakout feature is not essential, as you can always set up parallel meetings by launching different sessions online.

RECURRING URLS

Many online meeting applications create URLs for meetings. Having *one* link to click on, rather than creating a different address for each individual meeting, makes life easier. You can even have different, recurrent URLs for different meetings (for example, for weekly catch-ups, monthly strategic sessions, etc.), to give you the illusion of going into different 'rooms'.

If you are not using a calendar to organise your meetings, then pin the URL in the relevant collaboration space, or add it to the description of the corresponding channel, so it is always easy to find.

RECORDING OPTION

There will be times when someone who really wants to be at a meeting can't be there, so it is good to have the option to record a meeting. (For guidance on whether you should record your meetings, see Chapter 23.) Tools which can record in the cloud make it easier to share the recording than those that record onto your computer or device – but remember that while cloud recording might be a useful feature, it can become a security risk.

EASY CUSTOMISATION

Many platforms allow users to set some default options, such as always having the camera on when joining a meeting.

If you are the host of the meeting, customise your settings so that attendees have as much control over how they turn up as possible. For example, some platforms allow you to set up meetings so that attendees' webcams switch on as soon as they join the meeting. This can surprise attendees, making them feel like they have joined the meeting unprepared.

The more attendees can gradually turn on and off their options, and the more control they have over how they show up – the more comfortable they can make themselves from the beginning of the meeting.

CUSTOMISATION OF VIEWING VIDEO

In the same way as how you sit in relation to each other in a room makes a difference to those present in the meeting, how we view others on the screen during an online session can influence how we engage with the group and the conversation. Some people like to see whoever is speaking 'in the spotlight', taking up most of the screen; while others prefer to view everyone's faces at the same time, to see how team members are reacting and maintain a sense of connection throughout the meeting (Figure 12).

In the same way, when someone is sharing a screen, some of you will prefer to see both screen and speaker, while others might prefer only one point of focus. Being able to choose between different ways of viewing others on your screen is definitely a plus.

Figure 12: Different video screens

HIDING YOUR OWN WEBCAM STREAM

In Chapter 35, I mentioned that one of the reasons that people resist using video in their online meetings is that they don't like to see themselves. A feature that allows attendees to hide their own video feeds is highly desirable. Even if this is of no use to you (because you like to check your own position and appearance over the webcam), other people in your team may find it useful.

SCREEN-SHARING

Also as mentioned previously, if you are holding regular meetings with your team, it's good to have an option where everyone (not just the host or presenter, as some platforms call the person starting the meeting) can share their screens. In some applications you can change the default settings in advance. However, in other platforms, the host has to hand over control to others during the meeting, which interrupts the fluidity of conversation. A feature that allows people to share their screen when they need to, without being granted 'special powers', is preferable.

Some applications even enable someone in the meeting to take control of another person's screen, which can be quite interesting (and fun) – although not very secure.

A WHITEBOARD OR SHARED ANNOTATING/DRAWING SPACE

Having a common place where everyone can scribble on can be handy. It's the equivalent of having a whiteboard that we can all walk over to, or a big piece of flip chart paper we can write on at the same time.

If you and your team members enjoy sketching out ideas, look for a platform with an integrated whiteboard, rather than having to pull up a separate tool. If you use the integrated option, check whether the drawings will be stored, or whether you will need to take a screenshot to save your sketches and notes.

MOBILE APPS

It goes without saying that whatever platform you decide to use should have a great mobile app to go with it. (Of course, there may be other options available in the future, but at the time of writing, this is what is available.)

EASY TO DIAL INTO BY PHONE

As we have already seen, not everyone in your team will have a solid internet connection all of the time. If people are in your team who move from location to location, or who need to travel for work, for those moments of dodgy connectivity you need a platform where people can easily dial in by phone.

AVATARS FOR PARTICIPANTS NOT ON WEBCAM

When I meet with a team using audio-only, or if some team members can't turn on their webcams, profile pictures help me feel connected to those in the meeting. I'm a very audio-led person (I prefer to hear rather than see you extremely clearly), but if I have a picture of you in front of me and am listening to your voice, I feel a stronger sense of connection than if I'm staring at a black screen or looking at my surroundings.

Just as I prefer a platform that shows someone's picture when they are not on video, it might also help you or some of your team members. Another little feature to look out for.

ABILITY TO JOIN THE MEETING BEFORE THE HOST

I remember hanging out outside the school classroom with my friends, waiting for the teacher to unlock the door to the room. Although I had turned up early to make sure I was at my desk, with my notebook open right from the start of the class (I was a very responsible child!), I wasn't able to settle down at my desk until the teacher opened the door.

I feel the same way when I turn up early to an online meeting to make sure my tech is in order, but I can't log on. I am greeted by a message such as: "The meeting can't start until the host logs on, and they're not here yet" – which means that if the host doesn't turn up until just before the meeting is due to start, I can't be completely ready for the start time.

Even though I have turned up early to make sure my sound is working and that my webcam is pointing in the right direction, I still end up checking my set-up once the meeting has started. At least when my classmates and I found the door to the classroom locked, we could still hang out and chat among ourselves.

When you turn up to an online meeting where the room is 'locked', unless everyone else also has their backchannel open, you can't even talk to others. Being able to have a meeting that anyone can join before the host has its advantages –so whenever possible, pick a platform that allows you to do so.

'PUSH TO TALK': INTEGRATING THE SPONTANEITY FACTOR

In the colocated space, some of our most valuable interactions take place spontaneously: in the corridor, by the toilet door (or even in the toilets!), by the coffee machine. While these interactions rarely come under the label of 'meetings', I don't want you to forget about them.

These spontaneous interactions are one thing that people miss most about not working in the same space as their colleagues. They are also where valuable information gets exchanged informally. The good news is that they can happen in the online space, but only if you have built the infrastructure for them. Think about it: in the physical office, those conversations that happen in corridors wouldn't happen if there weren't any corridors. And there are plenty of office spaces which have been carefully designed to encourage people to have serendipitous encounters, by placing the coffee machine or other 'attractors' in strategic locations.

Do you have a space where your team members can 'bump into' each other? For example, can they see when others are logged onto a platform, or even when they are editing a document or task card? Collaboration software is evolving in such a way that we can see whether someone is working on the same platform, and at the same time, as us. Those are chance encounters. Sometimes seeing that someone is there with you will establish a sense of connection.

On top of that, when you see that someone is on the same site as you, you might suddenly realise that you need something from them. If it's easy to hop on a call of some kind with them, you'll reach out. However, if you need to leave your desk, go into a meeting room with the necessary equipment, send them an invitation to a meeting room, etc., you probably won't bother. The moment has passed.

As you choose your collaboration tools, look for those with a 'push to talk' option, or one-click access to an audio or video call. It will help you and your team members have richer conversations day-to-day.

<u>41</u>

The kit wrap-up

Be aware of your posture during your meetings. It will affect how you feel about them.

Find a set-up that helps you be as comfortable as possible (for example, wireless headsets, adjustable desks). Avoid meeting on the move.

Take a break between other work and your meetings. Think of stepping into a meeting. Clear your desktop of unnecessary windows and tabs, and take breaks away from the screen when possible.

Be aware of how you look and sound. Customise your background to suit you and your meeting. Hide your own video, if it helps you concentrate on others.

Learn to master the tech to create the best meeting experience possible.

Have a backchannel and a back-up plan for when the tech doesn't work as well as it should.

Identify the platform features most useful to you, and either pick a platform to best suit your needs, or customise what you already have as much as possible.

For a list of how the current meeting platforms meet my recommendations, head over to onlinemeetingsthatmatter.com.

Coda

Did you ever think that a book on running online meetings could be this long?

I never knew that online meetings could play such an important part not only in helping teams work well together, but also in helping us advocate for a more flexible approach to work.

Back in May 2017, I attended a conference on activity-based working where professionals gathered to discuss how best to design workspaces that allowed people to find the best environments in which to work.[96] All through the conference I kept hearing from speakers and the floor that remote work would never be as good as 'real work', because we are social animals and need social interaction. I bit my tongue many times on that day, and I wonder whether all that repression ignited the little spark that eventually became this book.

No, I don't think that meeting people online is always as comfortable as meeting them in-person. But once you get used it, you can build strong connections by meeting people on video online (and through audio-only too!), as long as you are having conversations about things that matter to you, and in a way that make you feel like you are not wasting your time.

Slowly, technology will catch up. Gradually, more and more organisations will reduce their floor space. Step by step, the world of work will adopt a much more flexible approach, throwing out of the window many practices that don't help us produce better work.

We will adopt healthy ways of collaborating with people we only see a few times a week, online.

We will no longer think about whether we are colocated or remote; we will just consider whether we need to change our communication ecosystems to work better together.

We will stop talking about 'tools', and just talk about our behaviour and our work. And eventually, we will stop having 'online meetings'.

We will just have meetings that matter.

---

96   To find out more about the Work 2.0 conference, listen to Virtual Not Distant (2017) 'WLP125: Work 2.0 Conference and redesigning workspaces', podcast, 8 June. Available at: www.virtualnotdistant.com/podcasts/work-2-conference

References

Adair, John (2009) *How to Grow Leaders: The Seven Key Principles of Effective Leadership Development*, Kogan Page (Kindle Edition).

Alexander (2007) 'Five weeeeeeeird for great meetings', *The Chief Happiness Officer Blog*, 20 February. Available at: https://positivesharing.com/2007/02/five-weeeeeeeird-tips-for-great-meetings/

Axtell, Paul (2018) 'The most productive meetings have fewer than 8 people', *Harvard Business Review*, 22 June. Available at: https://hbr.org/2018/06/the-most-productive-meetings-have-fewer-than-8-people

Bluedorn, Allen C., Turban, Daniel B. and Love, Mary Sue (1999) 'The effects of stand-up and sit-down meeting formats on meeting outcomes'. *Journal of Applied Psychology* 84(2): 277–285.

Businessballs (2019) 'Mehrabian's communication theory: Verbal, non-verbal, body language'. Available at: www.businessballs.com/communication-skills/mehrabians-communication-theory-verbal-non-verbal-body-language/.

Dr Karl (2012) 'Can walking through a doorway make you forget?', *ABC Science*, 21 February. Available at: www.abc.net.au/science/articles/2012/02/21/3436001.htm

Duhigg, Charles (2016) *Smarter Faster Better: The Secrets of Being Productive*, Random House (Kindle Edition).

Duvall, Jeremey (2016) 'Our current process for handling feedback', 5 October. Available at: https://jeremey.blog/sparta-feedback-process/

freistil IT (2017) 'Working out loud doesn't mean being noisy', 23 December. Available at: www.freistil.it/working-out-loud/

Fried, Jason (2016) *ReWork: Change the Way You Work Forever*, Ebury Publishing (Kindle Edition).

Fried, Jason and Heinemeier Hansson, David (2018) *It Doesn't Have to Be Crazy at Work*, HarperCollins (Kindle Edition).

Garber, Stella (2016) 'How to give your team meetings a status update', Trello, 14 April. Available at: https://blog.trello.com/give-team-meetings-status-update

Gartner (2017) 'Remote workers tend to work longer hours, UK Study finds', 11 October. Available at: www.cebglobal.com/talentdaily/remote-workers-tend-to-work-longer-hours-uk-study-finds/

Gascoine, Joel (2020) 'A simple guide to better coaching and feedback in your company', Buffer. Available at: https://blog.bufferapp.com/a-simple-guide-to-better-coaching-and-feedback-in-your-company

GitLab (nd) 'GitLab Communication: Random'. Available at: https://about.gitlab.com/handbook/communication/#random-room

Gonda, Victoria (2020) 'What happened when our team switched to only asynchronous meetings', Inside Buffer. Available at: https://open.buffer.com/asynchronous-meetings/

Hall, Kevan and Hall, Alan (2017) *Kill Bad Meetings*, Nicholas Brealey Publishing (Kindle Edition).

Hanselman, Scott (2015) 'Tragedies of the remote worker: "Looks like you're the only one on the call"', 16 March. Available at: www.hanselman.com/blog/TragediesOfTheRemoteWorkerLooks-LikeYoureTheOnlyOneOnTheCall.aspx

Hassell, Martin D. and Cotton, John L. (2017) 'Some things are better left unseen: Toward more effective communication and team performance in video-mediated interactions'. *Computers in Human Behavior* 73(August) 200–208. Available at: www.sciencedirect.com/science/article/pii/S0747563217301966

Jay, Antony (1976) 'How to run a meeting'. *Harvard Business Review* 54(2): 43–57.

Kaner, Sam (2014) *Facilitator's Guide to Participatory Decision-making*, John Wiley & Sons.

Keith, J. Elise and Sutherland, Lisette (2019) 'Can your meeting kit cut it?', *InfoQ*, 3 September. Available at: www.infoq.com/articles/can-your-meeting-kit-cut-it/

Keller, Scott and Meaney, Mary (2017) 'High-performing teams: A timeless leadership topic', *McKinsey Quarterly*, June. Available at: www.mckinsey.com/business-functions/organization/our-insights/high-performing-teams-a-timeless-leadership-topic?cid=other-eml-ttn-mkq-mck-oth-1801

Kline, Nancy (2002) *Time to Think*, Cassell Illustrated (Kindle Edition).

Kopprasch, Carolyn (2020) 'One daily team meeting, across 5 time zones: Buffer's May happiness report', Buffer. Available at: https://open.buffer.com/buffer-may-happiness-report/

Laborde, Gant (2018) 'Virtual meetings have types', Infinite Red, 29 March. Available at: https://shift.infinite.red/virtual-meetings-have-types-4a13b3744639

Lydia M. (2015) 'How 15 minutes each week keeps our distributed team connected', Trello, 19 August. Available at: http://blog.trello.com/how-15-minutes-each-week-keeps-our-distributed-team-connected/

McChrystal, Stanley, Silverman, David, Collins, Tantum and Fussell, Chris (2015) *Team of Teams: New Rules of Engagement for a Complex World*, Penguin (Kindle Edition).

McGonigal, Kelly (2009) 'Change your posture', *Psychology Today*, 5 October. Available at: www.psychologytoday.com/gb/blog/the-science-willpower/200910/change-your-posture

McNulty, Eric J. (2017) 'How to maximize meetings', *Strategy + Business*, 10 July. Available at: www.strategy-business.com/blog/How-to-Maximize-Meetings

Maljković, Nenad (2016) 'Virtual team quick guide', Medium.com, 6 August. Available at: https://medium.com/virtual-teams-for-systemic-change/virtual-team-quick-guide-95736861e4ab

Mann, Annamarie (2017) '3 ways you are failing your remote workers', Gallup, 1 August. Available at: www.gallup.com/opinion/gallup/214946/ways-failing-remote-workers.aspx

Meyer, Erin (2016) *The Culture Map: Decoding How People Think, Lead, and Get Things Done Across Cultures*, PublicAffairs (Kindle Edition).

Misener, Dan (2017) 'How a sticky note could make you more productive at work', *CBC News*, 4 April. Available at: www.cbc.ca/beta/news/technology/videoconferencing-workplace-productivity-1.4053566

Mroz, Joseph E. and Allen, Joseph Andrew (2015) 'It's all in how you use it: Managers' use of meetings to reduce employee intentions to quit'. *Consulting Psychology Journal* 67(4): 348–361.

Penenberg, Adam L. (2010) 'Social networking affect brains like falling in love', *Fast Company*, 1 July. Available at: www.fastcompany.com/1659062/social-networking-affects-brains-falling-love

Pentland, Alex (2012) 'The new science of building great teams'. *Harvard Business Review* 90(4): 60–70.

Perlow, Leslie A., Noonan, Hadley, Constance and Eun, Eunice (2017) 'Stop the meeting madness: How to free up time for meaningful work'. *Harvard Business Review* 95(4): 62–69.

Pink, Daniel (2018) *Drive: The Surprising Truth About What Motivates Us*, Canongate Books.

Pullan, Penny (2016) *Virtual Leadership: Practical Strategies for Getting the Best Out of Virtual Work and Virtual Teams*, Kogan Page.

Ressler, Cali and Thompson, Jody (2011) *Why Work Sucks and How to Fix It: The Results-only Revolution*, Portfolio.

ReWork (nd) 'Guides: Identify dynamics of effective teams'. Available at: https://rework.withgoogle.com/guides/understanding-team-effectiveness/steps/identify-dynamics-of-effective-teams/

Riordan, Christine M. (2013) 'We all need friends at work', *Harvard Business Review*, 3 July. Available at: https://hbr.org/2013/07/we-all-need-friends-at-work

Rothman, Johanna and Kilby, Mark (2019) *From Chaos to Successful Distributed Agile Teams: Collaborate to Deliver*, Practical Ink.

Scott, Kim (2017a) *Radical Candor: How to Get What You Want by Saying What You Mean*, Macmillan (Kindle Edition).

Scott, Kim (2017b) 'Small talk is an overrated way to build relationships with employees', *Harvard Business Review*, 25 July. Available at: https://hbr.org/2017/07/small-talk-is-an-overrated-way-to-build-relationships-with-your-employees

Settle-Murphy, Nancy (2012) *Leading Effective Virtual Teams*, Routledge.

Settle-Murphy Nancy (2019) 'Great global meetings: Navigating cultural differences', *InfoQ*, 30 August. Available at: www..infoq.com/articles/navigating-cultural-differences/

Settle-Murphy, Nancy (nd) '120 Essential Tips for Leading Amazingly Productive Virtual Teams'. Available at: www.guidedinsights.com/tips-guides

Sigillito Hollema, Theresa (2019) 'Don't waste a cultural bridge!', Interact, 5 March. Available at: www.interact-global.net/category/working-across-cultures/culture-cubes/

Sijbrandij, Sid (2017) '"Virtual coffee" breaks encourage workers to interact like they would in an office', *Quartz at Work*, 6 December. Available at: https://work.qz.com/1147877/remote-work-why-we-put-virtual-coffee-breaks-in-our-company-handbook/

Sullivan, Wendy and Rees, Judy (2008) *Clean Language: Revealing Metaphors and Opening Minds*, Crown House Publishing.

Sutton, Bob (2014) 'Why big teams suck: Seven (plus or minus two) is the magical number once again', *Work Matters*, 3 March. Available at: http://bobsutton.typepad.com/my_weblog/2014/03/why-big-teams-suck-seven-plus-or-minus-two-is-the-magical-number-once-again.html

Tannenbaum, Arielle (2020) 'A guide to conquering remote work loneliness from remote workers around the world', Buffer. Available at: https://open.buffer.com/remote-work-loneliness/

Wiseman, Liz (2017) *Multipliers: How the Best Leaders Make Everyone Smarter*, HarperCollins.

World Health Organization (2014) 'Safe surgery saves lives: Frequently asked questions', August. Available at: www.who.int/patientsafety/safesurgery/faq_introduction/en/

Acknowledgements

This is going to sound a bit like an Oscar speech, I have so many people to thank in this book! I'll start with thanking you, the reader, for adopting online collaboration practices – I'm sure you are helping to make the world of work a better place.

First off, if I have named you in the book: thank you for either sharing your experiences with me, or putting information and narratives out there for which others can make good use. Thank you to Mark Kilby, Nenad Maljković and Sharon Dale for their contributions through a conversation in Virtual Team Talk.

Big thanks go to all those beta readers who read the first draft of this book, especially because that version was definitely not ready to be shared. I completely changed the structure of the book, but incorporated many of their thoughts. In particular, I would like to thank Sarika Kharbanda, François Moscovici, Jonathan Norman, Penny Pullan, Melanie Pürschel and Sophie Segal for their detailed comments. I was very touched to get amazingly detailed feedback from Nancy Settle-Murphy. Thanks to Bart van Roey for using an early draft of the book to help with a workshop – it made me think that some of the stuff was indeed useful!

I learned a lot from guests of the *21st Century Work Life* podcast (thank you so much for all your time), and also from my days at Happy Melly (now Management 3.0), the first modern virtual team with which I worked. Members of the Virtual Team Talk online community have also contributed plenty to the content: thank you to you all, especially those in the #about_writing channel, and especially Theresa Sigilito-Hollema.

Thank you to my workshop participants, and the remote work advocates and distributed organisations who share all their thinking and practices on the web. I'm sure their stories and examples have made the text more entertaining than if I had simply shared advice on my own. I have also learned much from Helena Gulliksson (who has led many online meetings), and Mark Kilby, both directly in conversation and through his writings, including his book. And of course, thanks must go to Lisette Sutherland, previous co-host of *21st Century Work Life*, who first immersed me in the world of online collaboration.

Huge thanks to Maya Middlemiss, collaborator over at *Virtual Not Distant*, for her early edits and suggestions.

I am also grateful to have taken Alison Jones' 10 Day Book Proposal Challenge. For a few years I had been thinking that I needed to write a book on managing remote teams, but during the challenge I had the idea for this book you are reading now. (At the time of writing, I'm getting ready to take the challenge again and develop the idea for *Adventures in Podcasting*.)

Big thanks to the professionals carried over from *Thinking Remote*: Manuel Barrio (cover), Simon Hartshorne (design) and Lisa Cordaro (copy-editor and beyond).

Kevin, my husband, never ceases to support my book writing and all other ventures. Even though he never reads the books, he listens to me talk about them (endlessly!).

Finally, thanks again to my mum for her unconditional support. She has read everything I've written.

About the author

After delivering leadership training face-to-face and facilitating team away-days, in 2010 Pilar Orti started to look for non-location-specific opportunities to help people develop. Wanting to visit her parents in Madrid more often, and having met her future husband in Amsterdam, meant that limiting her work to her London base was no longer an option.

In 2013, she landed a freelance job with a training company, delivering accredited management and leadership qualifications online. There, she began to ignite discussion on the company forum and growing its webinar programme. Far from finding the shift to the online space daunting, Pilar quickly adapted her ability to create a sense of purpose and unity to the online space, and in 2016 she set up Virtual Not Distant.

Seeing as we spend more than 70% of our waking time at work, Pilar is fascinated by the opportunities that technology brings to make the world of work a better place. As well as trying to improve the working world, she is a serial podcaster and loves to write. She is the co-author (with Maya Middlemiss) of *Thinking Remote: Inspiration for Leaders of Distributed Teams* (Virtual Not Distant, 2019) and author of *The A to Z of Spanish Culture* (The Spanglish Project, 2014), *Thriving Through Change at Work* (Unusual Connections, 2014), as well as other volumes. She is the host of Virtual Not Distant's *21st Century Work Life* and *Management Café*, and is the co-host of *My Pocket Psych* and the International Association of Facilitators England and Wales' chapter, *Facilitation Stories*. In the solo show *Word Maze*, she talks about her process of writing a novel.

Pilar is an established voiceover artist: her credits include the voice of 'Xuli' in the CBeebies animation series *GoJetters*. She has turned her voiceover stories into the memoir, *Hi, I'm Here for a Recording: The Ordinary Life of a Voiceover Artist* (Paperplay, 2017).

Stay in touch with Virtual Not Distant

Do you have any questions about *Online Meetings that Matter*? Any thoughts or anecdotes you would like to share?

I would love to hear from you. Just head over to the contact form at onlinemeetingsthatmatter.com, and get in touch. You will find additional resources there too.

If you are looking for more reading material on leading remote teams, check out our collection of articles published as the book and audiobook, *Thinking Remote: Inspiration for Leaders of Distributed Teams*, or head over to Virtual Not Distant's blog (www.virtualnotdistant.com/blog) for our latest posts.

For all you podcast listeners out there, we cover a whole range of topics on leading remote teams and online collaboration in our show *21st Century Work Life*, which you can find in all podcast apps, as well at Virtual Not Distant's website.

Finally, at Virtual Not Distant we offer training for managers of remote teams, facilitation of team away-days for organisations making the transition to 'office-optional', and other services and products.

If you would like to work with us, head over to our website: www.virtualnotdistant.com